MARCO POLO

Tips

SRI LANKA

CHINA

PAKISTAN NEPAL BHUTAN

Tropic of Cancer BANGLADESH

VN

Mumbai INDIA BURMA LAOS

Arabian Bay of THAILAND
Sea Bengal

SRI LANKA

Colombo

www.marco-polo.com

The best Insider Tips → p. 4

INSIDER TIP

The West Coast → p. 32

The South → p. 46

The Highlands → p. 60

SYMBOLS

INSIDER TIP	Insider Tip
★	Highlight
●●●●	Best of ...
☼	Scenic view
☺	Responsible travel: fair trade principles and the environment respected

PRICE CATEGORIES HOTELS

Expensive	over 18,000 SLRs
Moderate	9,000–18,000 SLRs
Budget	under 9,000 SLRs

The prices are for a night in a double room without breakfast

PRICE CATEGORIES RESTAURANTS

Expensive	over 2200 SLRs
Moderate	1500–2200 SLRs
Budget	under 1500 SLRs

The prices are for a three-course meal without beverages

On the cover: From Colombo to Badulla by train p. 103 | Cycle around Polonnaruwa p. 83

CONTENTS

The Cultural Triangle → p. 74

The East Coast → p. 88

The North → p. 96

Road atlas → p. 124

DID YOU KNOW?

MAPS IN THE GUIDEBOOK

(126 A1) Page numbers and coordinates refer to the road atlas
(0) Site/address located off the map
Coordinates are also given for places that are not marked on the road atlas
Maps of Colombo, Anuradhapura and Kandy can be found inside the back cover

INSIDE BACK COVER: PULL-OUT MAP →

PULL-OUT MAP 〽

(〽 A1) Refers to the removable pull-out map
(〽 a–b 2–3) Refers to additional inset maps on the pull-out map

The best MARCO POLO Insider Tips

Our top 15 Insider Tips

INSIDER TIP Nostalgically stylish

Dutch Hospital in Colombo Fort is one of the trendiest locations on the island. The complex has a number of good restaurants, chic boutiques and pleasant cafés → p. 36

INSIDER TIP The elephant's meeting place

More than 150 wild elephants gather around the reservoir in the Minneriya National Park in July and August – the months with low rainfall → p. 82

INSIDER TIP A bit fishy

Hard on the nose, but a treat for your eyes: in Negombo one of the largest fish markets in the country opens in the early hours of the morning → p. 43

INSIDER TIP Right on trend: wake-boarding

You can try out this exciting water sport in the area near the mouth of the Ging Oya River north of Negombo → p. 45

INSIDER TIP Dolphins ahoy!

Hundreds of dolphins frolic in the sea off the coast of the Kalpitiya Peninsula. If you are lucky, you might even see some whales → p. 44

INSIDER TIP Turtles on the beach

Almost every night, sea turtles come on to the beach in Rekawa to lay their eggs. Dressed in dark clothes, you can accompany the environmentalists and watch the action → p. 57

INSIDER TIP Where Alec Guinness got wet

The world-famous 'Bridge on the River Kwai', with Alec Guinness in the main role, was filmed on the Kitulgala in 1956. Now you can go rafting on the same river → p. 69

INSIDER TIP Made in Sri Lanka

The Odel Luv SL in the Queens Hotel on Dalada Veediya in Kandy has a great selection of chic dresses, fabulous accessories and colourful souvenirs from Sri Lanka → p. 66

BEST OF ...

FOR FREE

● *Jungle feeling in the Cultural Triangle*
Buddhist monks used to live in the *Ritigala Strict Nature Reserve*. Today, the remains of their hermitages are surrounded by dense jungle. Enjoy the atmosphere while it is still free → p. 82

● *Enchanted temple*
The *Nalanda Gedige*, a more than 1000-year-old Buddhist sanctuary between Matale and Dambulla, has an idyllic location on the edge of a reservoir. You will not only be able to admire the landscape here but also spare your wallet: entrance is free (photo) → p. 81

● *Colourful world of the gods*
The *Sri Muthumariamman Thevasthanam* in Matale is one of the most important Hindu temples in the region. You can skip the entrance fee as the most interesting part of the holy place is the exterior where the figures on the facades seem to be straight out of a Hindu picture book → p. 69

● *Tea tasting*
In contrast to most of the other tea plantations, there is no charge for the guided tours and tea served at *Mackwood's* in Labookellie. Stock up on tasty teas and other souvenirs in their shop → p. 65

● *Glittering gems*
Amethysts, rubies and emeralds – the *Gem Bank & Gemmological Museum* has dozens of temptations in store for you – you will be delighted even if your jewellery box is already overflowing and it doesn't cost anything to have a look → p. 73

● *Grey giants at no cost*
If you want to see wild elephants in the national parks, you will have to dig deep into your pockets to pay the entrance fees. That is not the case in the *Lahugala-Kitulana National Park*. There, you will be able to admire the pachyderms free of charge from the A4 national road; they usually gather around the reservoirs → p. 91

●●●● Dots in guidebook refer to 'Best of ...' tips

● *Sri Lanka on the tip of your tongue*

The first culinary highlight of the day is a typical Sri Lankan breakfast. Especially tasty string hoppers — lacework of noodles made with rice flour — various curries and other delicacies are served in the Veranda Restaurant of the *Galle Face Hotel* in Colombo → p. 41

● *Lush tropical flair*

Experience the botanical diversity of this tropical island on a stroll through the *Peradeniya Botanical Gardens* near Kandy. More than 4000 different plant species and 10,000 giant trees flourish on the 153 acre complex (photo) → p. 69

● *Pilgrimage in airy heights*

At an altitude of 2243m (7359ft) *Adam's Peak* may not be the highest mountain on Sri Lanka but it is the most sacred. Take your place in the endless stream of pilgrims to see the spectacular sunrise over the mountain landscape from the summit. However, to do this, you will have to leave the comfort of your bed just after midnight → p. 71

● *Elephant processions in the winter*

These take place every year at full moon in January in the *Kelaniya Raja Maha Vihara*, a Buddhist place of pilgrimage in the east of Colombo, and around the *Gangaramaya Monastery* in the heart of the island's metropolis on the full moon night one month later → p. 39

● *A hike to the end of the world*

Your hike on *Horton Plains*, a high plateau that is a UNESCO World Heritage Site, will take you through a unique landscape of rhododendron bushes and tree ferns and, if the weather is fine, you will have a wonderful view of the plain below from *Land's End* → p. 72

● *Drummed to prayer*

Three times a day traditionally dressed drummers summon visitors to the one-hour ceremony in the famous *Temple of the Tooth* in Kandy and the faithful stream to the open shrine on the first floor to pay honour to the relic — one of Buddha's eyeteeth → p. 65

ONLY IN

BEST OF ...

● *Negombo's rustic coffee house*
When the monsoon clouds start to roll in, the *Icebear Century Café* in Negombo is the perfect place to take shelter and weather the storm over coffee and cake → p. 43

● *Shopping in the KCC*
Browse for clothing in the branches of Sri Lankan companies such as Odel, Hemeedia and Ranjanas, or look for literature in the Vijitha Yapa Bookshop, in the *Kandy City Centre (KCC)* (photo) → p. 66

● *Ignore the highland weather in style*
The weather in Nuwara Eliya is often rather British: rainy and cold. That is when the *Road Hole Bar* in the Jetwing St Andrews is a good place to relax and enjoy a whisky in front of a crackling fire or play a game of billiards on the more than 120-year-old table → p. 70

● *Artistic and culinary delights*
The *Serendipity Arts Café* in Galle not only serves delicious coffee and tasty dishes but also has books for you to browse through and artworks to admire. The time you spend waiting for the sun to shine again will pass in a flash → p. 51

● *A visit to the gods*
Tourists only rarely visit the *Museum* that is overshadowed by the monuments in Polonnaruwa. Unjustly; it not only shows the importance and development of the former royal city but is also the home of beautiful bronze statues of Hindu deities → p. 85

● *Cinema fun in the Regal*
You will probably not understand a single word spoken in the Sri Lankan blockbusters, but the atmosphere in the 1930s *Regal Cinema* will transport you back to Colombo's good old days → p. 40

RAIN

RELAX AND CHILL OUT
Take it easy and spoil yourself

● *Ayurvedic relaxation*

Be pampered in Ayurvedic style in the pleasant atmosphere of the branches of *Spa Ceylon* where each treatment becomes something of a ritual. The wellness and beauty products also make great little gifts → p. 40

● *Meander through a tropical idyll*

Brief Garden near Bentota is not only a highlight for fans of all things botanical. It is also a fine place to go for a stroll and get a sense of the tropics. As guests of the artist Bevis Bawa (who died in 1992) Laurence Olivier and Agatha Christie also strolled through here → p. 50

● *A meditative holiday*

The *House of Lotus* in Dodanduwa, south of Hikkaduwa, is the right place to give a spiritual touch to your holiday. This can be achieved through a balanced diet and meditation courses – and the beach is just around the corner → p. 56

● *Ravana's hot tears*

The *hot springs of Kanniyai* near Trincomalee bubble up where Ravana, the legendary ruler of the demons in the Ramayana, once shed his tears over the abduction of Sita. The local people believe that the water has healing powers and that it brings prosperity → p. 94

● *A lagoon cruise*

Enjoy a boat trip through the *Rathgama Lagoon* near Dodanduwa with its colourful birdlife and mangroves. The atmosphere is especially lovely in the early morning or at sunset when the sun bathes the area in gentle hues → p. 56

● *Buddha and I*

The *Aukana Buddha*, a standing statue carved out of the rock, is one of the masterpieces of artistic creativity. Soak up the atmosphere of contemplation and tranquillity (p h o t o) → p. 80

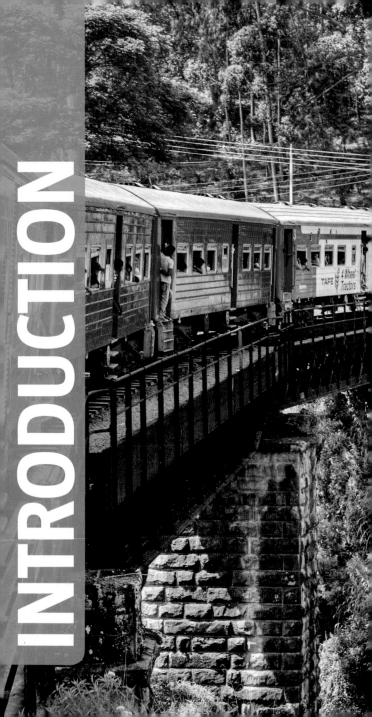

INTRODUCTION

DISCOVER SRI LANKA!

On the map, Sri Lanka looks like a tear-shaped emerald dangling below the Indian subcontinent. Here, on this tropical island not even 700km (435mi) from the equator, the lush green of the groves of rustling palm trees and dense jungle forests mixes with the bright green of rice paddies and tea plantations. No other county in the world has been given so many beautiful names by its visitors: the Romans called it *Tabropana*, the copper-coloured, more than 2000 years ago and Arab seafarers named the island *Serendib*, the enchanting. Ancient Sanskrit writings refer to it as *Sinhala dvipa,* the lion island. The name the county has borne since 1972, *Sri Lanka*, is also poetic; it means the venerable beauty although the Tamils still call it *Ilankai*, the wonderful.

Covering an area of 25,300mi², Sri Lanka may be small but it displays all of its legendary bio-diversity in the 435km (270mi) from Point Pedro in the north to

Photo: A train ride through the mountains

Close to paradise: a palm-fringed beach on Sri Lanka's western coast

Dondra south of Matara. The widest distance from east to west is 225km (140mi) but the wealth of natural richness on this small island is quite astonishing. The 1300km (800mi) of coastline has endless sandy beaches and remote bays with coconut palms swaying in the breeze and steep rocky coasts. Tourists can enjoy the water all year round; between November and April in the west and deep south and from May to October on the east coast, where there is more accommodation now that the civil war has ended. No matter whether you decide on a simple guesthouse, an elegant colonial villa or chic resort – you will find exactly what you are looking for on the island's long beaches. The civil servants of the British Empire looked longingly out to sea from Mount Lavinia, while Sri Lanka's oldest beach resort Negombo started

attracting holidaymakers from Europe in the early 1970s. Tourists will find something to satisfy all tastes along the so-called Gold Coast between Colombo and Galle. Water sport enthusiasts, as well as those who just want to have a relaxing holiday, will be delighted with everything that is on offer here while those who venture out into the hinterland will be well rewarded with secluded lagoons, peaceful lakes and enchanted tropical gardens. Arugam Bay in the east, in turn, attracts surfers from all over the world as the surf spots are among the best in Asia while divers can enjoy the depths of the Indian Ocean with reefs teeming with sea life and historic shipwrecks.

And that is not all. The cardamom bushes, pepper vines and cinnamon trees founded Sri Lanka's fame as a spice island, while palm groves, rice paddies and rubber plantations still play an important agricultural role today. In 1911, Herman Hesse was euphoric after one of his strolls in the mountains and penned: 'This is where we find paradise with the abundance and richness of all its natural gifts'. As with the famous author of 'Siddhartha', tourists today go into raptures during their highland trips: tea plantations cover the mountain slopes like green carpets, unspoiled

Travellers are in raptures

mountain villages such as Ella and Haputale have spectacular panoramic views and there are wonderful waterfalls such as the Dunhinda Falls and wild rivers like the Kitulgala. The scenic mountains are not only a contrast to the coast; they also have completely different climates. No matter where you go, you should be sure to have

1658–1796	1802	1942	After 1948	1956–59
The Dutch V.O.C. trading company has a monopoly of power; in the heartland of the Kingdom of Kandy	The island becomes the British Crown Colony of Ceylon. Expansion of the plantation economy	Trincomalee bombed by Japanese troops	Democracy with changing governments	Increase in Singhalese nationalism at the expense of the Tamils

a windcheater and pullover with you at all times. Sri Lanka's national parks also make it a major destination for lovers of nature. Wild elephants around the reservoirs, leopards in the savannah, troops of monkeys between temple ruins and schools of dolphins in the open sea – they can all be spotted through your binoculars.

Remains of a highly developed culture

The ancient cities in the Cultural Triangle hark back to a highly developed civilisation that is over 2300 years. This not only resulted in the stone witnesses to Buddhism but – due to the low rainfall in the dry areas of the country – also a sophisticated irrigation system. Many of the 33,000 reservoirs in Sri Lanka today were established during the era of the old kings. The motto of the great 12th century ruler Parakramabahu – who had thousands of canals and reservoirs set up and restored – was: 'No matter how small the drop of rain, it should not flow into the sea without first benefitting man'. Today the reservoirs are important biotopes for water birds and wild elephants, many of them, including Minneriya and Kaudulla, are in the middle of vast nature reserves.

If you wander through the areas of ruins in the former royal cities of Anaradhapura and Polonnaruwa, or climb up to the spectacular Sigiriya mountain fortress, you will get an idea of the skill and artistry of the early inhabitants by looking at the monuments they left behind. Ancient stupas – known as *dagobas* in Sri Lanka – rise from the wide plains and remind one of the difficult paths from Samsara to Nirvana. Finely crafted Buddha statues exude an inner peace and serenity that not only touch the devout viewer. The dazzling colours of the bare-breasted 'cloud maidens' in Sigiriya have delighted visitors for over 1500 years. The multicoloured Hindu temples create a completely different, less contemplative, impression. Their tall gate towers are covered with sculptural depictions and seem more like a 3-D picture book. Here the gods and goddesses cavort alongside the demons and legendary creatures from the mythological Hindu universe. There are wonderful examples in Colombo and Matale and no shortage of them in Jaffna and Trincomalee, which are once again accessible.

But it was on this island, so richly endowed by nature and blessed with countless temples and sanctuaries of peaceful philosophies, that the opposite took place. A bloody civil war that lasted from more than a quarter of a century – from 1983

1960
Sirimavo Bandaranaike becomes the world's first female head of government

1983
Outbreak of the ethnic conflict with tens of thousands of deaths

26 December 2004
More than 35,000 killed by tsunami; global assistance

2009
After a campaign lasting many months government troops succeed in ending the civil war

2013
Boom in tourism and high economic growth rates

to 2009 – took the lives of tens of thousands of people and deeply divided the society. The conflict between the Singhalese majority and members of the Tamil minority hung like a leaden cloud over the country. This ethnic conflict may have something to do with the Singhalese foundation legend: Vijaya, the son of a North India king and grandson of a lion (*sinha* in Singhalese), landed on the island with 700 warriors and became the founding father of the Singhalese (lion people). In the 3rd century BC, a son of the great Indian Emperor Ashoka converted the King of

The Sigirya Rock rising from the plain

Anuradhapura to Buddhism. Since that time, the religion of the Enlightened has determined everyday life and, with its festivals, the annual rhythm of the majority of the population. But, the Hindu Tamils have been on the island for just as long as their brothers. Most of the time, they lived a life of peaceful coexistence although there were frequent struggles for political power and wars. However, the Tamils were given preferential treatment during

Buddhism determines the everyday life of most Sri Lankans

the British colonial days until the Singhalese elite turned the tables following independence in 1948. In 1983 the pent up distrust exploded in a wave of violent unrest that resulted in a long civil war.

Today, more than ever, the Sri Lankans are wonderful hosts that delight in showing visitors their home and welcome them warmly with both a Singhalese *ayubowan* and Tamil *vanakklam*.

WHAT'S HOT

1 Safari in style

Adventure Animal enthusiasts and nature lovers do not have to forgo any creature comforts. Although you will be sleeping in a tent in the *Mahoora Luxury Safari Camp (www.mahoora.lk)*, it is splendidly equipped – it even has a bed. *Leopard Safaris (www.leopardsafaris.com)* serves an elegant dinner under the starry skies. It almost makes you want to spend the night outside in a hammock. The *Kulu Safari Company (www.kulusafaris.com, photo)* sets up its dining tables at the most beautiful spots imaginable.

East meets west 2

Music The country's many influences can be heard in its music – Bollywood rubs shoulders with hip-hop, the guitar harmonises with the flute. Those who don't already know the rapper *M.I.A. (www.myspace.com/mia, photo)* you soon will as she is Sri Lanka's most famous musician. *Bathiya and Santhush (bnsmusic.com)*, with their fusion sound, are other real stars. *Clancy's (29 Maitland Crescent | Colombo)* is a good place to hear live music.

3 On the water

Active Trick skiing, knee boarding and wake skating: these are the water sports of the hour. Those who want to be really hip can take an acrobatic or barefoot course *(Pi-Mono-Sport | Kaluwamodara Alutgama)* or swish across the water on their knees off the coast of Bentota (courses and equipment in the *Ayurveda Hotel Paradise Island | www.ayurvedahotelparadiseisland.com* and *Hotel Saman | Aturuwella | www.samanvilla.com)*. For the right look fashion-conscious water sport enthusiasts can shop at the *A Frame* beach shop run by *Mambo Surf Tours (Hikkaduwa)*.

Imported from Nippon

Sushi There is definitely no lack of fresh fish and seafood in Sri Lanka. But until recently, sushi was almost completely unknown. The locals remained faithful to their strongly spiced foods and are only now slowly starting to discover tempura, yakitori and sushi. *Nihonbashi (Alexandra Place 5 | Colombo)* and *Sakura (Rheinland Place | Colombo)* are recommended for these Japanese delights. The *Ginza Hohsen (in the Hilton | Sir Chittampalam A. Gardiner Mawatha | Colombo | www.ginzahohsen.com)* is extremely elegant and renowned for its teppanyaki.

4

Creative art

Fashion For many years, Sri Lanka has served as a production site for international fashion labels. Nowadays an increasing amount of clothing is being designed in the country itself. Fair trade fabrics and organic materials play a major role and the result is not just an eco-linen blouse but the kind of modern clothing that also looks at home on the streets of New York, London, Paris or Berlin. The sustainable lingerie line *Charini (Duplication Road | Colombo | www.charini. com)* produces seductive undergarments that can be worn under outfits by designers such as *Ruchira Karunaratne (www.face book.com/ruchira.karunaratne)*, *Rebel (www.facebook.com/RebelColombo)* and others. New labels and names are being added to this list all the time. It is a good idea to have a look at the participants of the *Sri Lanka Design Festival (www.srilankadesign festival.com)* and the graduates of the *Academy of Design (www.aod.lk, photo)*.

5

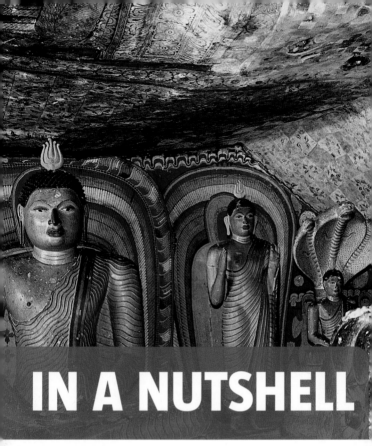

IN A NUTSHELL

BUDDHISM

The overwhelming majority of the Singhalese follow the 2500 year old teachings of Siddhartha Gautama. Born into a noble family in North India, Gautama undertook a search for meaning following a young life of self-indulgence. Meditating under a fig tree *(ficus religiosa)*, he became the Buddha, the Enlightened, who recognised a causal connection between desire and suffering that can only be changed by the removal of desire and the longing for immortality. Man can reach the state of Nirvana, the complete extinction of desire, by following the 'eightfold path' and in this way end the cycle of reincarnation. The faithful strive to achieve as much good karma as possible by making donations, giving alms to the monks, and following the five moral laws (do not kill, do not steal, do not commit any sexual transgressions, do not lie and do not take any intoxicating substances).

CEYLON

Although the country's former name was done away with in 1972, it is still present in many places. For example, *Ceylon Tea* is still one of the country's internationally famous brands. The term can be traced back to the Chinese *Xi Lan*

Photo: In the cave temples of Dambulla

Buddha's own island – with coconut palms and elephants, environmental protection in its infancy and stunning nature

that Marco Polo's writings introduced to mariners' circles as *Seilan* and a corruption of the Sanskrit word *Sinhala Dvipa*, island of the lion people. In the 16th century the Portuguese named the island *Ceilão*.

The Dutch then called it *Ceylan* before it became Ceylon under the British. The name was retained for many years after independence.

COCONUT PALM

On arrival in Colombo by ship in 1925, the famous Indologist Wilhelm Geiger noted that: 'As far as the eye can see, to the north and to the south, it is fringed with coconut plantations.' And today, many regions in Sri Lanka are still dominated by these palms. The trees that are synonymous with being on holiday for European tourists are one of the most

Tourist magnet: elephants in the Pinnawala orphanage

valuable crops for the locals. Close to 6 per cent – almost 1600mi² – of the total area is covered with coconut trees. Along with tea and rubber, coconut is one of the main items of export. There seems to be no limit to the coconut palm's usefulness: the trunk is used to build houses and boats, the fronds for roofing and material for weaving, and the fibres of the outer nutshell are use in the making of ropes, mats and brushes. Cups, spoons and other utensils are made from the hard shell of the coconut. It is also impossible to imagine Sri Lankan cooking without the coconut: most curries have the flesh – known as *kobra* – as one of the ingredients. Is there anything better than the fresh juice of a yellowish-green king coconut or the high-proof Arrack made from distilled palm juice as an after-dinner digestive? Not to mention a relaxing massage with the soothing oil of the pressed *kobra*.

DAGOBA

Massive Buddhist religious building, usually in a bell or semi-spherical shape. The origin of the Singhalese word *dagoba* can be traced back to the Sanskrit *(dhatu and gharba)* and means reliquary shrine. Reliquaries are objects that – actually or according to legend – have a connection with Buddha.

ELEPHANTS

In Sri Lanka elephants are venerated and represent wisdom and strength. More than 5800 elephants live in the wild and nowhere in Asia can one see them in such great numbers as in Sri Lanka (especially in the Minneriya, Kaudulla and Uda Walawe National Parks). Only 150 animals are used as working elephants. It is considered an honourable deed to either lend or donate strong elephants to the monasteries for their main processions; more than 50 animals take part in the famous *Kandy Perahera*. However, their natural habitats are threatened and this – along with their predilection for bananas, rice and sugar cane – has led to them regularly invade large fields and gardens. In the attempts to drive them out, around 50 people and 200 marauding pachyderms lose their lives every year.

ENVIRONMENTAL PROTECTION

Plastic waste on the roadside, exhaust belching cross-country buses, dirty beaches – the tropical paradise is anything but a poster child for environmental protection. But the growing number of environmental organisations shows that a change in thinking is slowly taking place. Some activities are also being undertaken in the tourism branch: for example, renowned hotel chains such as Aitken Spence and Jetwing have set high ecological standards for their hotels. In fact, there is actually a long tradition of protecting nature in Sri Lanka. As early as the 3rd century BC, King Devanampiya Tissa forbade any kind of hunting in the area around Mount Mihintale. 1500 years later, a ruler in Polonnaruwa did something similar and made killing any living creature in the vicinity of his royal city a punishable offence. The British colonialists were responsible for the greatest exploitation of nature. Excessive big-game hunting and clearing enormous areas to create tea and rubber plantations had such a devastating effect that the colonial government gave the areas of Yala and Wilpattu protection status in 1938. Today, around 13 per cent of the country has been declared reserve areas.

FLORA & FAUNA

The leopard stretches out contentedly in the warm sand. He doesn't seem to be bothered at all by the frenzied clicking of the tourists' cameras and the jeeps not far away. The savannah-like Yala West National Park in the far southeast of the country is famous for its comparatively high leopard population. More than 40 specimens make their tracks through the dry bush land, where sloth bear and sambar deer are also at home. Those more interested in birdlife will not have to travel much further. The lagoons in the nearby Bundala National Park are a haven for countless water birds including groups of pink flamingos. Sri Lanka is a fabulous destination for ornithologists – more than 400 bird species have been counted and 33 of them can only be found here.

As a result of its extremely varied landscape, Sri Lanka offers astounding biodiversity. Where else is it possible to see the world's two largest mammals – elephants and blue whales – on the same day? To do this, you will have to set out to sea from Mirissa early in the morning to the area where blue whales are regularly sighted. In the afternoon, you can then wind through the Uda Walawe National Park where it is estimated that 700 elephants are on the move.

When you feel that you have seen enough of the lush jungle landscape in the Sinharaja Forest Reserve, you can drive past teak and mahogany plantations into the mountains to admire the wide expanses of magnificent rhododendron bushes and tree ferns on the Horton Plains. Even when you visit the old royal cities it is likely that you will come across quite an array of wildlife amid the ruins. Four of the five species of monkeys endemic to Sri Lanka – including the cheeky toque macaque and the grey or Hanuman langur – can be spotted in Polonnaruwa alone. On the way back to your hotel, you might meet up with another animal resident of the island; in spite of being more than three feet long, the Bengal monitor lizard is completely harmless.

GEOFFREY BAWA

On Sri Lanka one name in particular is associated with contemporary architecture: Geoffrey Bawa. The influential architect, who died in 2003 at the age of 83, designed some of the most interesting

Rich harvest – palm with coconuts

buildings on the island including the New Parliament (opened in 1982) and the University of Ruhuna in Matara. But, his most spectacular is the Heritance Kandalama Hotel near Dambulla which nestles into a mountain ridge and seems fused into the jungle. This is a prime example of Bawa's legendary ability to create a unity between architecture and surrounding nature. One of his most im-

portant tenets was that buildings should be able to be experienced with all of the senses and this made him one of the most important representatives of the so-called 'tropical modern' in Asia. Unlike many other architects, Geoffrey Bawa had a feeling for the character of a specific location. This can also be seen in his Jetwing Lighthouse Hotel, which stands majestically on a rocky rise on the coast at Galle and references colonial stylistic elements in its architecture. Some of his early hotel buildings, including the Heritance Ayurveda Maha Gedara – that opened as the Neptune Hotel in Beruwala in 1976 – have been lovingly restored by his pupils. Almost 50 years after his first hotel was created in Negombo in 1965, its ruins were transformed into the luxurious Jetwing Lagoon. Additional information can be found under: *www.geoffreybawa.com*.

HINDUISM

The young Tamil girl smashes the fibrous coconut on the floor of the temple with all her force and the coconut water flows out of the broken shell. What appears to be an outburst of violence has an ancient tradition in Hinduism where the coconut symbolises human existence and shattering it represents inner cleansing. Around 15 per cent of the entire population embraces Hinduism; most of them are Tamils. The Indian religion is especially prevalent in the northern and eastern parts of the island. Some of the Hindu gods also play an important role for Buddhists as protectors of the island, and there is hardly any Buddhist monastery that does not also have a small Hindu shrine – known as *devale* – on its grounds. The Hindus are united in their belief in the principle of the eternal cycle of creation and destruction. They are also convinced that their individual self takes on a new form after their death. What they are reborn as depends on their karma, the deeds they performed during their lifetime. The abstract idea is of a Supreme God represented by an army of gods, sprits and demons that are honoured as the individual chooses. Shiva is far and away the most popular Hindu god; in the form of a lingam he is the symbol of fertility, as a cosmic dancer he represents destruction but he is also revered as an ascetic. Many temples are also dedicated to his son Skanda, who is known as Murugan and Katagaram as the god of war, and is considered the powerful protector of the island.

MOONSTONE

One name for two completely different things: the shimmering semi-precious stones of feldspar and a semi-circular stone slab in religious Buddhist architecture that travel guides like to refer to as a 'holy foot mat'. They mark the transition from everyday surroundings to a sacred space. Animal motifs symbolise the four stages of human life: birth (elephant), sickness (lion), old age (bull) and death (horse). The lotus in the centre is the symbol of purity and leads to the five steps to enlightenment and, in this way, into the temple.

SINGHALESE

Three quarters of the approximately 21 million people in Sri Lanka belong to this demographic group. The Singhalese use an Indo-Aryan language and writing and trace their origin back to the legendary Prince Vijaya. The first Singhalese probably migrated to Sri Lanka from the northern part of India a good 2500 years ago. King Devanampiya Tissa embraced the religion of Buddha in the third century BC and laid the foundations for the highly-developed Sri Lankan culture in the Cultural Triangle and they have regarded themselves as the guardians of this religion and the leading national group on the island since that time. With the exception of some Christians (principally fishermen near Negombo) most of the Singhalese are Buddhists. Following independence, the nationalist 'Sinhala only' policy of the then Prime Minister S.W.R.D. Bandaranaike, who wanted to install Singhalese as the sole national language, resulted in the first major conflict with the Tamil minority. Now that the war has ended, many Singhalese are making efforts to achieve a peaceful form of coexistence with the island's minorities.

TAMILS

The second-largest demographic group (around 17 per cent) originally came from South India. They speak a language that belongs to the Dravidic family and is not at all related to Singhalese. Two large groups with very different histories live on the island. The so-called Sri Lankan (or Jaffna) Tamils – who make up about 12 per cent of the population and have been part of the island's history for almost as long as the Singhalese – have their settlements in the north and east. There are also slightly more than 1 million Indian (or highland) Tamils in the mountains who mainly live on the tea plantations. Their forebears – mostly members of lower castes – were brought to the island by the British in the 19th century to provide cheap labour on their plantations. Today, they are still at the bottom of the income ladder. There is little contact between the two groups and the Indian Tamils were not involved in the military conflict for an independent Tamil state (Tamil Eelam) fought by the Tamil Tigers since 1976. More than 80 per cent of the Tamils are Hindus and the remaining percentage are Christians.

FOOD & DRINK

The traditional cuisine of the island has many diverse influences – Indian, Arabic, Malay – that all find their way into the nation's bowls, pans and plates and the end result is curry.

The former colonial powers – Portuguese, Dutch and, least of all, the British – have left their traces in many of the recipes. Curry and rice – that sums up just every local meal. It is extremely tasty, easy to digest and, when compared with European prices, very inexpensive, and is also often a feast for the eyes.

Sri Lankan curry has nothing in common with the instant spice that is sold at home. Curry refers to both the mixture of ground spices – some of which are roasted beforehand – as well as the dish itself. There is usually a choice between a vegetable curry, beef, chicken or – less common – pork curry.

Especially in the countryside, colours are commonly used to describe the various curry dishes. A white curry is based on coconut milk and is mild and almost as liquid as a soup. Red curries have large amounts of chilli (similar to our cayenne pepper). Black curries are the most common and contain roasted coriander, cumin and fennel. The roasting process releases the aroma out of the spices and roasting the spices is what distinguishes

Whether you go for the hot curries or the fresh seafood – either way it will be a delicious culinary experience

Sri Lankan curries from those made in neighbouring countries especially the Indian varieties that are much better known at home.

Chilli – dried or as a powder – is the hottest spice. There are many different varieties of chilli – green and red, big and small, fat and thin. Pickles are just as popular as they are in Indian cooking: they are usually served as a side dish, such as *seeni*

sambola. That is a special mixture that includes chilli (powder), as well as garlic, cardamom, dried shrimps, ginger and tamarind paste.

Depending on what is being prepared – and how the cook is feeling – cinnamon, cloves, nutmeg and other spices are added to this basic mixture. The curries are served in several bowls that are brought to the table at the same time. The food

LOCAL SPECIALITIES

FOOD

▶ **abba** – spicy mustard; popular as an accompaniment to meat or spread on a sandwich

▶ **appé** – pancakes made with rice flour, yeast and coconut milk; often also called hoppers

▶ **bandakka curry** – vegetarian dish of okra; very popular in the highlands

▶ **breudher** – yeast cakes of Dutch origin

▶ **ghee** – clarified butter; important in Ayurveda cooking

▶ **jackfruit**– extremely nourishing tree crop; prepared as sweet, aromatic fruit (photo right) or as starchy vegetable

▶ **kaha bath** – yellow rice cooked in coconut milk; for festive meals

▶ **kiribath** – milk rice with grated palm sugar and/or cinnamon

▶ **lampries** – rice cooked in meat broth, filled with minced meat and baked in banana leaves

▶ **paripoo** – Ceylonese style lentil dhal, accompaniment to tuna fish and tumeric, often served with curries

▶ **pattis** – small pastries; traditionally served at birthdays but now also a popular party snack

▶ **rasagullas** – coconut milk dumplings (dessert)

▶ **rathu isso** – shrimp curry (the small shrimps are cooked in their shells)

▶ **rotis** – flatbread, made with grated coconut or coconut flakes in Sri Lanka; popular at breakfast

▶ **wattalapam** – pudding made with palm-flower sugar, coconut milk and spices – usually cinnamon

DRINKS

▶ **arrack** – liquor made with the fermented sap of coconut flowers

▶ **curd** – a type of yogurt made from buffalo milk

▶ **coconut milk** – juice from the yellowish-green king's coconut, very refreshing (photo left)

is often served lukewarm and the Sri Lankans will not understand if you make any complaints about this. You mix your portion of rice with the side dishes: lentils, aubergines, cucumbers and breadfruit, as well as meat and/or fish and seafood. Pappadams – light, crispy, flat wafers made from lentil flour – are always served along with curry and no meal would be complete without one or more chutneys. The condiments are used to add more tang or – in the case of sweet chutneys – to reduce the heat. The finely grated coconut flakes that are also always on the table fulfil the same purpose of cooling the palate. Tropical Sri Lankan fruits – papayas, mangos, small aromatic bananas and pineapples – always complete the meal.

INSIDER TIP Try a Ceylonese breakfast. Hoppers – light, bowl-shaped pancakes made of rice flour, coconut milk and coconut flakes –, are something very special in the morning. The dough is drawn into thin threads to make string hoppers. If two eggs are fried on top of the pancake, it is known as an egg hopper. Buffalo-milk curd and palm honey *(kitul)* accompany the hoppers.

Chilli sambolas – spicy sauces made with dried shrimp or fish and chilli powder, onion and oil – are also part of a traditional Sri Lankan breakfast.

Most holidaymakers look forward to the selection of fresh fish and seafood. No place in Sri Lanka is more than 130km (81mi) from the coast and this means that there is also often fish and seafood on the menu of the hotels in the highlands. It is great fun to eat grilled jumbo prawns, tasty seer fish (a mackerel variety) or a curry of fried squid or lobster with garlic sauce at beach restaurant, with your feet in the sand, surrounded by palm trees with the starry skies of the tropics above. The light local beer (Three Coins and Lion Lager) is fairly good and the tea, which is always available and usually served with milk, is excellent. In contrast, the coffee served in most restaurants leaves a lot to be desired. However, there are an increasing number of cafés with professional coffee machines that are helping to remedy the situation.

A fine selection of sweets, as well as fruit, is served for dessert. *Aluwa* was brought into the country by Arab immigrants; it is a mixture of sticky rice, palm sugar, cashew nuts, coconut milk and various spices. Muslims from the Malayan-Indonesian

Traditional dish: chicken curry

world contributed *wattalapam,* a caramelised pudding of coconut milk and cashews, to the island's cuisine. *Thalaguli*, sugary sesame balls, and *bibikkan*, rice cakes with different flavours, will also appeal to those with a sweet tooth. Before you eat too much *puhul dosi*, sweet, preserved pumpkin, you should make sure that you have arranged an appointment with your dentist.

The Tamils brought a great variety of snacks with them from South India. In best Sri Lankan English, these are known as short eats and include *roti*, stuffed pancakes, *thairu vadai*, turnovers filled with yoghurt and *parripu vadas* red lentil fritters.

You will usually have no trouble in satisfying your hunger on Sri Lanka as most of the eateries are open from morning until night.

SHOPPING

Sri Lanka, which is often seen as coming close to paradise, may not quite be the Garden of Eden for tourists used to the shopping in Thailand or Hong Kong. Here, you will not be offered the mass of counterfeit 'brand name' goods and it is also not the place to look for bargains in the electronics field. But the island does have a long tradition of diverse arts and crafts making it easy to fill your suitcase with any number of small souvenirs. The largest selection can be found in Kandy (antiques, arts and crafts, jewellery, batiks and tea). Government shops have fixed prices and opening hours but most of the small merchants stay open until late in the evening and also on Sundays. However, it is not only their opening times that are somewhat irregular: you will have to bargain if you are interested in buying. As a rule of thumb, you should never pay more than 70 per cent of the original asking price.

ARTS AND CRAFTS

Arts and Crafts Centres, as well as the government-run *Laksala* shops offer a good overview but the carvings, coconut fibre, ceramic ware, lacquer boxes, ashtrays and trays, as well as various textile products (batik fabrics, woven and lace cloths, and wall decorations) seem rather outdated and boringly traditional. It is a better idea to buy handicrafts in private shops and studios. In many places, you will also be able to see how the items are made. Galle and the south coast are famous for their lacework and Ambalangoda is renowned for the carved masks produced there.

COSMETICS

Perfumed oils, soaps and creams produced locally are popular gifts to take home with you. The pharmacies have the widest selection. That is also where you can buy the legendary balm produced by the *Siddhalepa* firm that is said to bring relief from colds, flu, headaches, toothache and common aches and pain.

GEMSTONES

Sri Lanka has a reputation as an island of jewels so you should be prepared for the temptations from gemstone dealers. The

Spices, colourful printed fabrics, scented oils and wooden elephants – souvenir hunters will not be disappointed

selection includes alexandrite, citrine, topazes, rubies, sapphires and emeralds from around Ratnapura. But be careful: if you are not an expert, you should only buy in the prestigious, larger shops and ignore all the tips given by the rickshaw drivers and touts, who are just after their cut (especially in Kandy).

HERBS AND SPICES

The cheapest place to purchase herbs, teas and spices is at the markets but the quality sold there is often substandard. This is especially true of tea. The *Keells* and *Cargills* supermarket chains have good quality for everyday use. Attractively packaged tea can be purchased in more expensive specialist shops such as the *Mlesna Tea Centre*. There are also the shops at the spice gardens and tea plantations in the highlands where high quality products are offered.

Arrack, which is available in pretty bottles, is another popular souvenir.

TEXTILES

A number of internationally famous companies produce goods in Sri Lanka so there are many places with an excellent selection of inexpensive clothing. This is especially true in the shopping centres in Colombo which include *Majestic* and *Liberty*, as well as the branches of *Odel* and *Fashion Bug*. Sri Lankan designers are also playing an increasingly important role and local labels, such as *Buddhi Batiks, Arugam Bay* and *Stringhopper* can be found in a colonial mansion at *32 Ward Place*. Ladies who want to dress in a chic south-Asian style will be happy with the selection of saris in the colourfully painted specialist shops while the *Bale Bazaar* in Nuwara Eliya is a good place to shop for warm jackets.

THE PERFECT ROUTE

THE WEST COAST AND COLOMBO

The capital city **1** *Colombo* → p. 34 is the ideal place to set out from to explore the island: take a stroll through the multicultural Pettah district and relax at the Galle Face Hotel with wonderful views out to sea. You will have the Indian Ocean in sight as you drive along the coastal road to the south. How about a day at the beach? One of the resorts near **2** *Bentota* → p. 46 is a good tip. You should also not miss out on making a slight detour to visit Brief Garden, a magnificent, enchanted tropical paradise. The historically important fort at **3** *Galle* → p. 50, with its defensive walls, quaint small streets and original cafés, is a real highlight.

THE FAR SOUTH

The trip continues along the south coast. You can make a stop in **4** *Mirissa* → p. 52 to take part in a whale watching tour and to enjoy the beach. This is also a great place to try out surfing. As you drive on, it is worth making a stop in Dondra near **5** *Matara* → p. 56 where a lighthouse (photo left) marks the southernmost point in Sri Lanka. **6** *Tissamaharama* → p. 54 is not only worth visiting for its historical importance but also because it is a good starting point for a safari in the **7** *Yala West National Park* → p. 54.

HIGHLANDS AND KANDY

Next up is a scenic drive to the northeast that takes you first via Wellawaya to the Buddhas hewn out of the rocks at **8** *Buduruwagala* → p. 63 and then on a winding road to **9** *Ella* → p. 60. The town offers a breathtaking panorama of the mountains and a view down to the Indian Ocean. You should start your trip on to the old British summer holiday retreat of **10** *Nuwara Eliya* → p. 69 , with fabulous colonial architecture, early in the morning so that you will also have time to visit the **11** *Horton Plains* → p. 72 and do a three-hour hike. The spectacular beauty of the highlands with its verdant tea plantations (photo right) unfolds as you proceed on your journey

Experience the many facets of Sri Lanka – the coast, the highlands, the Cultural Triangle – and a detour to the east

towards ⑫ *Kandy* → p. 63, Sri Lanka's last royal city and the site of the island's most sacred shrine and its famous tooth reliquary.

THE CULTURAL TRIANGLE

The route now continues, on through a lush tropical landscape with interesting spice gardens, into the heart of the Cultural Triangle. Look for accommodation near ⑬ *Sigiriya* → p. 86 so that you will be able to get up early and have the colourful frescoes with the 'cloud maidens' to yourself. A visit to the ⑭ *Minneriya National Park* → p. 82 will give you the chance to see some elephants. After that, make a detour to the royal city ⑮ *Polonnaruwa* → p. 83. Park the car and explore the expansive complex of temple ruins by bicycle.

DETOUR TO THE EAST

After visiting all of these ancient sights, you will probably feel like going for a swim in the sea. Absolutely no problem; just take the A 11, you will be in trendy ⑯ *Kalkudah and Passekudah* → p. 92 within a few hours. After your dip in the ocean, travel northwards along the east coast to ⑰ *Trincomalee* → p. 93. The town with the famous natural harbour also has some beautiful beaches and a colourful Hindu temple.

FINALE IN NEGOMBO

You will have to drive across the island once again to reach the final destination of this route. It is more than 240km (150mi) to the seaside resort of ⑱ *Negombo* → p. 43 where you will be able to relax. Halfway, you can stop at ⑲ *Dambulla* → p. 81 to admire the beautiful cave temples full of Buddhas.

1200km (745mi). Travel time: 30 hours
Recommended duration: 14 days
A detailed map of the route can be found on the back cover, in the road atlas and on the pull-out map

THE WEST COAST

Sri Lanka's largest urban area spreads out extensively on the west coast between the Negombo Lagoon and Colombo's southern suburbs of Mount Lavinia and Moratuwa and reflects both the beauty and variety, as well as the problems, of the country.

On the trip into the city from the Katunayake Airport, near the fishing and resort town of Negombo, visitors are greeted by views of lush tropical vegetation. The traffic becomes heavier and more chaotic as you approach the centre. Cyclists, pedestrians and three-wheel tuk-tuks, which are usually called trishaws here, all weave their way between the cars. The cityscape has changed a lot in recent years and the new skyscrapers are the most obvious sign of this.

The juxtaposition of pulsating modernity, exotic hustle and bustle and green oases makes Colombo an extremely interesting place for a holiday or stopover. However, the churches – mostly Catholic – in and near Negombo are reminders, not always peaceful, of the missionary activities of the Portuguese.

Retracing the footsteps of the Dutch can make interesting excursions: to the so-called 'Cinnamon Canal', the Christian cemeteries in the dunes and the old manor houses of that era. You will learn

Photo: Boats on the beach in Negombo

Temples, churches and beaches – the booming capital city and its surroundings bring back memories of the colonial period

more about the life of the fishermen, the fascinating landscape and the country's aquatic gems on an excursion to the Negombo Lagoon or the open sea on a traditional outrigger boat.

The west coast north of Colombo is a flat stretch of land divided by numerous waterways with rivers such as the Kelani Ganga, which flows into the Indian Ocean on the northern outskirts of Colombo, and lagoons like the one in Negombo. On many days – particularly in the morning – the coastal region is covered with a haze mixed with smog. However, if the view of the hinterland opens up, you will be able to see the cone of a mountain that is considered sacred in many religions: *Adam's Peak,* the historical landmark of travellers on their way to the legendary island of jewels.

Buildings from the colonial era alongside modern skyscrapers in Colombo

COLOMBO

MAP INSIDE BACK COVER
(136 A1) (*ᗢ B14*)
More than 2 million people – almost one tenth of Sri Lanka's population – live in Colombo and its suburbs.

> **CITY** **WHERE TO START?**
> **Dutch Hospital**: The classic means of transport in Colombo is the three-wheeler tuk-tuk (with taximeter, 50 SLRs/km). You should take one to the Dutch Hospital opposite the World Trade Center in the Colombo Fort and then set out to discover the city's colonial flair along York Street and the streets leading off it, before heading towards Pettah.

The city, which was an important stopover point on the way to the Far East in the era of the British Empire, experienced a long period of security problems but has now developed into one of the towns with the most promising futures in Asia. The present is even more exciting: a get-up-and-go feeling and new hopes are apparent in many areas and walks of life. Young scenes are springing up in the cultural and, especially, culinary realms and it will be worth your while to spend a little time discovering Colombo at leisure with an experienced guide. The city has variety of spectacular buildings and almost all of them bear witness to the city's turbulent past with its various colonial powers.

The Portuguese were the first to fortify Colombo – its name probably comes from *kolamba,* the Singhalese word for harbour – at the beginning of the 16th century. However, Colombo's rise only began around the middle of the 17th century when the Dutch expanded their control over Ceylon's cinnamon plantations. The appearance of the city was most influenced by the British. From the end of the 18th century until the day independence was granted on 4 February 1948 the British determined the fate of the tropical island from their headquarters in Colombo. Since then it has developed a skyline that has pushed the old colonial palaces into the background. The towers of the World Trade Center, the Bank of Ceylon and other skyscrapers can even be seen from the terrace of the Mount Lavinia Hotel, an hour's drive south.

SIGHTSEEING

DUTCH PERIOD MUSEUM

The inscriptions on the tombstones in the peaceful courtyard of the more than 300 year old building in the heart of Pettah, which has been a museum since 1982, make visitors aware of the hard – and often very short – lives of the colonial merchants. Furniture made of tropical wood and ivory, and documents, maps and pictures are also on display. *Tue–Sat 9am–5pm | entrance fee 500 SLRs | 95 Prince Street*

FORT DISTRICT ⭐

The fort walls used to jut out into the sea but the walls were demolished in 1872. Unfortunately, security risks make it impossible to visit some of the most important sections. This also applies to the lighthouse, which was built in 1857, the old post office and former governor's residence – today, the seat of the country's president – on Janadhipathi Mawatha. They all from part of a High Security Zone and off limits. Where Sir Baron Jayatillake Mawatha meets York Street is *Cargills*, the oldest department store in Colombo. The store used to supply the tropical clothing needed by the planters, officers and colonial

---

⭐ **Fort District**
The oldest department store in Colombo and the legendary hotels are reminiscent of the British era
→ p. 35

⭐ **Colonial Colombo**
The magnificent white colonial buildings around the National Museum and Town Hall not only delight travellers with a love of nostalgia → p. 37

⭐ **Pettah**
Pure Asia: the Muslim bazaar district with its narrow streets and amazing shops, Hindu temples and mosques is ideal for strolling, browsing and bargain hunting → p. 38

⭐ **Galle Face Hotel**
A favourite location for travellers looking for a bygone era, and those who enjoy a sophisticated high tea
→ p. 41

⭐ **Dutch Canal**
The Cinnamon Canal near Negombo – a 120km (75mi) long, lively idyll from days gone by – and also a perfect destination for cyclists → p. 42

⭐ **Kelaniya Temple**
Wonderful Buddhist temple complex near Colombo where the faithful lay fresh flowers in front of the statues every day. The temple is the site of a spectacular Perahera at full moon in January → p. 42

MARCO POLO HIGHLIGHTS

Colombo locals meet at Galle Face Green – even when the weather is less than perfect

civil servants. It is a good idea to take a break in the renovated legendary *Grand Oriental Hotel* on the corner of York and Church Streets. As the name says, you will have a splendid overview of all the activity going on below from the ⚓ *Harbour View Restaurant* on the 4th floor of the hotel. The atmosphere in the former INSIDER TIP *Dutch Hospital* between Hospital Street and the World Trade Centre is a mixture of nostalgia and trendiness. The tastefully renovated buildings of the 17th century hospital now house restaurants, boutiques, cafés and a branch of Ceylon Spa.

GALLE FACE GREEN

Especially at the weekend and on full moon days, this strip of land along the seaside is one of the most popular meeting places for Colombo locals: children fly their kites, their parents and young people go for a stroll, buy ice cream or roasted nuts, go for a swim or watch jugglers perform

their tricks. Tourists are welcome here; they will often be approached but usually in an inquisitively friendly manner.

INDEPENDENCE MEMORIAL HALL

The Duke of Gloucester opened the first session of the Ceylonese Parliament in the open Independence Hall – constructed in the style of ancient royal audience halls – on 4 February 1948. The reliefs on the walls depict scenes from the country's history and there is a monument of the first Prime Minister, Dudley Shelton Senanayake, in front of the hall. The historic site is a popular meeting place for young people.

The *Bandaranaike Memorial International Conference Hall* is just a few steps away; the modern building is a gift from the People's Republic of China and was built in 1973 to commemorate Prime Minister Solomon Bandaranaike who was murdered in 1959. *Daily | free admission | Independence Avenue/Maitland Place*

COLONIAL COLOMBO ★

You will enjoy a feeling of nostalgia when viewing the administration buildings in the Fort district and the old hotels but also the magnificent white buildings around the National Museum and Town Hall. The *Mayor's House* (the former library) and the *Parliamentary Guesthouse* are particularly fine architectural examples. The *Museum*, with the statue of Governor Sir William Gregory (1872–77) in front of it, and the *Town Hall*, built in the style of the Capitol in Washington in 1927/28, are located diagonally opposite. The interface between modern and exotic Colombo can be seen at the corner of Main Street and Gaswork Street Junction, the striking Moorish-style building is the beautifully renovated INSIDER TIP *Old Town Hall*. This was where the destiny of the city was determined from 1873 to 1928. After that, the council and administration moved to the *Town Hall* on Vihara Maha Devi Park, formerly Victoria Park. If you are prepared to give a tip (around 150 SLRs.) you will be able to take a look at a surprising room on the first floor. A group of men can be seen sitting around a table; they include the spokesmen of the Singhalese, Tamils and Muslims, as well as burghers of Dutch origin, and there is even an Englishman there – his name is W. Shakespeare. What makes this meeting so special is that the gentlemen are actually life-like wooden sculptures (and the British man was actually called W. Shakespeare; shown on the photograph hanging next to the wooden figures). The former *market hall* is right next door.

MARRIAGE ANNOUNCEMENTS

'Well-off parents, father professor, Govigama Buddhist, are looking for a slender, presentable wife for their son, 27, 1.75m, non-smoker, software engineer. More information on our family and our son's horoscope under MG 7194'. This is a typical example of the hundreds of announcements that are printed in all the Sunday newspapers. Reading these announcements offers insights into the importance of status and social relevance of the Sri Lankan middle class and 'better circles'. Looking for a bride or a good catch for the daughter balance each other. It is always the parents, mother or family who contact any future children in law; the young people never make their wishes known to the public.

The old town district of Pettah has been strongly influenced by the Muslim and Tamil merchants

NATIONAL MUSEUM

Surrounded by gigantic banyan trees the white colonial style building is a major sight in itself. Finds from Sri Lanka's ancient past are displayed in Gallery II, religious art from the historic royal cities of Anuradhapura (III) and Polonnaruwa (IV), as well as art (and gifts of state from around the world) from Kandy (VI and VII) and other sites, especially from the Cultural Triangle region, are exhibited in Gallery V. A small hall has a display of Buddhist symbols and provides and interesting introduction to the most important religion in the country. There is also a comprehensive library and collections of artistic craftwork and folk art. *Daily 9am–5pm | entrance fee 500 SLRs, photo fee 1000 SLRs (!) | Sir Marcus Fernando Mawatha*

PETTAH ★

The colourful bazaar district is dominated by Muslim and Tamil merchants. The area is bounded by the harbour, train station and bus terminus and is only a short walk away from the Fort via the Main Street. A clock tower marks the entrance to the district where you will find many guild streets: *Gabo Lane* is the place to go for (mainly eastern) Ayurvedic natural medicine while *Sea Street* is almost completely dominated by jewellers with their small, mirrored shops. Several Hindu temples (the most interesting: *Sri New Kathiresan Kovil* on Sea Street is dedicated to Skanda, the god of war) and mosques (*Jami ul Alfar, 2nd Cross Street/Bankshall Street,* a 1909 red and white brick building with a clock tower is the most photographed) all give Pettah lots of oriental flair. The market is at its liveliest between 10am and midday and after 4pm.

SEEMA MALAKA AND GANGARAMAYA

Seema Malaka juts out into the Beiral Lake like a small island. The simple three-part wooden pavilions belong to Ganaramaya Monastery on the opposite side of the street and, with their Buddha figures and bodhi tree, exude a tranquil atmosphere. Monks are ordained in the main hall, which was erected in1978. Every year at full moon in February a ● spectacular procession with monks, dancers and elephants makes its way through the streets to the Gangaramaya Monastery for *Navam Poya*. *Daily 5.30am–11pm | entrance fee 100 SLRs | Sir James Peiris Mawatha*

WOLFENDAHL CHURCH

Wolfendahl Street (also written as Wolvendaal) makes its way upwards from Pettah through the old Dutch Quarter to a hill with the best-preserved Dutch Reformed Church in the country. It was built on the foundations of a Portuguese church in 1749. There are no official visiting hours but there is usually somebody in the adjacent school building who will open the church for you. The main attractions include the old christening and wedding registry, the 400 year old Dutch bible, the baptismal font support carved out of tamarind wood, the governor's chair and the organ. *A 150–200 SLRs tip is appropriate*

FOOD & DRINK

CRICKET CLUB

This is a great venue in the trendy Kollupitiya district – especially at lunchtime: reasonably priced light dishes including good pasta and salads and service that is just as friendly as the – mostly young – guests. A popular meeting place for ex-pats living and working in Colombo. The café restaurant is decorated in keeping with its name with many cups and posters. *34 Queens Road | tel. 011 250 13 84 | Moderate–Expensive*

INSIDER TIP DELI MARKET

The upscale snacks are very popular with the office workers in the area near the 39-storey World Trade Center (WTC) in the city. The Deli Market has a wide selection that includes Italian, Chinese, Indian and Thai barbecue stands: an ideal opportunity to have a conversation with local executives who all speak excellent English. The food is first rate and inexpensive. *Level 3 in the World Trade Center on Echelon Square*

INSIDER TIP FLAG & WHISTLE

This restaurant on the 5th floor of the Setmil Building has lovely panoramic views of the harbour. Its high ceilings and large windows give it a chic and spacious feel. The traditional German cooking and Asian specialities are a delight and the pub and beer garden are institutions in Colombo. Sporty, casual clothing is the accepted dress code. *256 Srimath Ramanathan Mawatha | tel. 011 248 55 00 | Expensive*

GALLERY CAFÉ

This is where the young and beautiful meet for dinner. They have no problems with the dim lighting just as long as they manage to get a place in the courtyard covered with tent-like lengths of cloth: very stylish, very trendy. The menu has both Mediterranean and Asian influenced dishes. *2 Alfred House Road | tel. 011 258 21 62 | Expensive*

PARK STREET MEWS

This popular restaurant is located in a pleasant side street to the east of Beira Lake. Good international cuisine from *biryani* to pasta is served in an old warehouse that dates back to the early 20th century. A tasty Sri Lankan breakfast is a highlight on weekends and Friday is the day for live music. *50/1 Park Street | tel. 011 230 01 33 | Moderate*

SHOPPING

You will find authentic small gifts typical of the country in the bazaar streets in Pettah. Although the interior of *Cargills,* the old colonial department store on York Street, is interesting for its nostalgic atmosphere, the selection of goods is somewhat stuffy. *Laksala,* next door is even fustier: more kitsch than good arts and crafts.

BAREFOOT

The articles offered by Barbara Sansoni, a well-known personality in Colombo, who is full of ideas and has impeccable taste, are a continual source of surprise. They include beautiful woven goods (such as placemats and cloths), charming little gifts (for example, notebooks with paper made of elephant dung), as well as a wide array of postcards and books on Sri Lanka; there is a bustling, shady garden café behind the shop. *704 Galle Road*

GEMSTONES

If you are lured into buying sapphires, moonstones and other glittering gems on the beach instead of in a reputable shop, you can have them valued and authenticated in the offices of the *Gem & Jewellery Exchange | 310 Galle Road* and the *World Trade Center | East Block, Nor. 27 A/2, Level 4 and 5*

MAJESTIC CITY

The best of Colombo's three large shopping centres (the others are the *Liberty* and *Unity Plaza*) is home to numerous shops selling textiles, books, tea and spices as well as the best cinema in town. *Galle Road*

ODEL

This shop has a wide range of tasteful goods that not especially expensive: fashion, shoes, jewellery as well as books, tea and tasteful souvenirs. *5 Alexandra Place*

INSIDER TIP PARADISE ROAD

This boutique in the heart of the Fort district sells high-end arts and crafts, antiques and some modern items, most of them made by local artists. A small bistro is also part of the complex. *213 Dharmalpala Mawatha*. A funky studio branch, with sales: *12 Alfred House Garden, next to the Gallery Café*

SELYN ☺

Buy lovely articles and support a worthy cause – this shop sells brightly coloured fabrics, dresses, toys and décor made from cotton produced by a women's initiative located near Kurunegala. *102 Fife Road | www.selyn.lk*

SPORTS & ACTIVITIES

REGAL CINEMA ●

The 1930s Art Deco cinema is an institution in Colombo. It usually shows Sri Lankan films and you will probably not understand very much but it is worth visiting the Regal just to experience the atmosphere. And, it is a good place to meet some of the locals. *8 Sir Chittampalam A. Gardiner Mawatha | tel. 011 2 43 29 36*

SPA CEYLON ●

At a Spa Ceylon you can choose between a massage, various Ayurvedic treatments, such as *shirodora,* or a body wrap. The spas are all in sophisticated surroundings such as the *Dutch Hospital* and the *Park Streets Mews*. Exclusive wellness and beauty products are also available to purchase. *Daily 10am–11pm | Dutch Hospital, Courtyard II | Hospital Street | tel. 011 2 44 19 31 and 5 66 66 63; Park Street Mews | 48D Park Street | tel. 011 5 34 00 11 and 2 30 76 76 | www.spa-ceylon.com*

ENTERTAINMENT

Although nightlife in 'Cool-ombo' cannot be compared with that in many other

Asian metropolises, there are still plenty of places where you can go out and have a good time. The well-established *Clancy's Pub (29 Maitland Crescent)* pulsates to sounds of local bands after 10pm on Fridays and Saturdays. *Rhythm & Blues (19/1 Daisy Villa Avenue/R. A. de Mel Mawatha)* is where local musician congregate. You will be able to listen to good live music almost every night there before heading off later to the INSIDER TIP *Club Mojo* in the *Taj Samudra Hotel* or the *Zouk Club* in the *Galadari Hotel*.

WHERE TO STAY

As Sri Lanka's most important business centre, Colombo has plenty of beds in the luxury and four-star category and an increasing number of stylish boutique hotels and villas. International hotel chains are also planning new projects. The *Hilton* is still considered the best establishment, followed by the *Cinnamon Grand,* the *Taj Samudra* and the *Cinnamon Lakeside*. Those who are looking for something more individual will find a good selection of stylish boutique hotels including the *Tintagel, Lake Lodge* and *Casa Colombo*. The hotels listed here combine nostalgic charm with modern comforts.

GALLE FACE HOTEL ★

The oldest home-away-from-home on the island was founded in 1864 and is a legend among colonial hotels. The Classic Wing is in the northern section and the more elegant Regency Wing in the south. No matter whether you stay in the hotel or not, every visitor to Colombo should try the ● lavish breakfast with delicious *string hoppers* or *High Tea* in the afternoon – both are served on the veranda – or go to the Checkerboard Bar for sundowners. Four bars, nine restaurants, shopping arcade, spa and large swimming pool. 147

rooms | 2 Galle Road | tel. 011 2 54 10 10 | *www.gallefacehotel.com* | *Expensive*

INSIDER TIP THE HAVELOCK PLACE

Artists and sophisticated travellers will feel at home in these two houses from the British colonial period that have been restored with great care. You can relax in the secluded garden with a pool and Jacuzzi and savour their homemade ice cream. 7 rooms | 6–8 Havelock Place | tel. 011 2 58 51 91 | *www.havelockbungalow. com* | *Moderate*

PARK STREET HOTEL

This 250 year old colonial villa close to Beira Lake has a very special charm – it comprises of twelve tastefully decorated rooms and suites with a swimming pool – a peaceful hideaway in noisy Colombo.

Colonial nostalgia: the Galle Face Hotel

A place to daydream: expansive views from the terrace of the Mount Lavinia Hotel

20 Park Street | tel. 011 5 76 95 00 | www.parkstreethotel-colombo.com | Expensive

INFORMATION

SRI LANKA TOURISM PROMOTION BUREAU
80 Galle Road | tel. 011 2 43 70 59 | www.srilanka.travel

WHERE TO GO

DUTCH CANAL ★
(132 A6, 136 A1) (*ⓜ B13–14*)

This waterway, which the Dutch constructed for the transport of cinnamon around 300 years ago, flows more than 120km (75mi) to the north as far as Puttalam. The approximately 25km (16mi) stretch of the Cinnamon Canal, from the capital city until just before Negombo, is the most interesting section: this is where people go fishing and swimming. The narrow road along the Hamilton Canal (named after the British engineer who fortified the shore) is the most pleasant side road to Negombo; it is also recommended for bicyclists.

KELANIYA TEMPLE ★
(136 A1) (*ⓜ C14*)

The beautiful Buddhist temple complex on the River Kelani only 10km (6mi) from the centre of Colombo is an impressive site of everyday faith. Only the Temple of the Tooth in Kandy and the large bodhi tree in Anuradhapura are more revered. The significance of the *Raja Maha Vihara* (Great Royal Temple) in Kelaniya can be traced back to a legend: it is said that Buddha himself sat on the throne that is preserved here under the white *dagoba*. The faithful lay flowers in front of the statue every day. A particularly large number of pilgrims come on full moon days. *Free admission*

MOUNT LAVINIA (136 A2) (*ⓜ B14*)

This beach and villa suburb in the south of the city, which is within easy reach by train, owes its fame to the eponymous hotel. The magnificent white building was built by Governor Thomas Maitland as his second residence in 1877 and *Mount Lavinia (226 rooms | 100 Hotel Road | tel. 011 2711711 | www.mountlaviniahotel. com | Expensive)* has been one of the most legendary colonial hotels in Asia for more than 100 years. The blockish extension built in the 1980s is really not attractive but one can still feel the atmosphere of the old British Empire throughout the hotel. You need only spend an afternoon on the ☆ pool terrace, with a view over the sea and of the skyscrapers in Colombo, and to confirm the magic this place exudes. The wide beach is not very long but is extremely well cared for. The popular INSIDER TIP *Boat Haus Café (37 Beach Road | tel. 011 2 73 27 55)* , which is only a stone's throw away from the hotel on the beach at Mount Lavinia, not only delights its guests with its relaxed seaside atmosphere but also with wonderful seafood dishes.

NEGOMBO

(132 A6) *(⌒ B13)* **The chequered career of a seaside town that, with its suburbs, has now grown into a large city with more than 100,000 inhabitants: this is where Sri Lanka's beach tourism began in the 1970s.**

For years, Negombo was thought of as a mediocre holiday destination for package tourists. However, in recent years efforts have been undertaken to improve quality and attract a more discerning public – with new hotels, an improved beach and sophisticated nightlife. Negombo is also a good place for a stopover at the beginning or end of a trip around the island because the airport is less than 10km (6mi) away. The expansive fishing settlement was developed into a trading centre by the Portuguese and Dutch and now attracts visitors with the liveliness of its colourful markets, as well as many churches and colonial buildings.

SIGHTSEEING

INSIDER TIP FISH MARKET

There is a great deal of hustle and bustle every morning until 11am at the fish market south of the entrance to the lagoon. In the afternoon, the traditional boats, *oruwas*, return to port with billowing sails – a popular motif for photographs. Worth visiting are the *Christian cemeteries* in the sandy dunes south of Negombo, the *Karawa settlements* on the island of Duwa to the north of the lagoon and the *Sunday market,* under trees with long trailing aerial roots, in the old fort that served as a prison for almost 200 years.

FOOD & DRINK

ICEBEAR CENTURY CAFÉ ● ◔

The more than 100 year old colonial building in the heart of Negombo is a vision in pink: the atmosphere in the interior is as stylish as in a Viennese coffee house and makes it an excellent location for a late breakfast or for a relaxed cup of coffee. Most of the products are Fair Trade and importance is given to taste and quality. There is also a good lunchtime meal. *25 Main Street*

INSIDER TIP OYSTERS

Sebastian worked as a chef in America for years before returning to take over his parents' business and investing it with new ideas: an open-view kitchen, crispy salads and the best hamburgers by far. This is also a popular location for celebrating private parties with guest DJs. *92 Poruthota Road, Ethukala | Mobile 0777 28 87 11 | Budget–Moderate*

ENTERTAINMENT

THE LORDS RESTAURANT
Fine Asian cuisine made with top quality seafood is served in chic surroundings, afterwards guests move to the bar or gallery for a nightcap. *80 B Poruthota Road (opposite the Hotel Jetwing Blue)*

RODEO
Pleasant watering hole with a Wild West theme; a meeting place for Europeans who live in the area. Good food (steaks) and good drinks. *35A Poruthota Road (between the Topaz and Jetwing Blue)*

WHERE TO STAY

THE ICEBEAR
The perfect place to chill out in tropical style. Eight cosy rooms and two holiday flats around a secluded garden. Ayurveda massages and the sea. And, if you feel like you must go somewhere else: bicycles are provided free of charge. *95/2 Lewis Place | www.icebearhotel.net | Budget–Moderate*

VILLA ARALIYA
Only a few minutes' walk away from the beach this resort offers 13 very elegant rooms and five holiday flats that are ideal for families. It also has a pleasant swimming pool and a good restaurant that serves delicious fish dishes and pizzas. *Kochchikade (5km/3mi north of the city) | tel. 031 2 27 76 50 | Moderate*

WHERE TO GO

KALPITIYA (128 A4–6) (*∅ B8–9*)
The Kalpitiya Peninsula, 130km (81mi) north of Negombo, separates the long Puttalam Lagoon from the open sea and there are plans to develop the peninsula along with the 14 islands in *Dutch Bay* into a luxury holiday destination. The first elegant resorts have already opened their doors. Attractive diving spots such as the *Reef Bar* and perfect waves for kite-surfing *(Kitekuda Camp | tel. 072 2 23 29 52 | www.srilankakiteschool.com)* make the region ideal for water sports enthusiasts. The sea off the coast of Kalpitiya is also the best place for INSIDER TIP ▶ watching dolphins – hundreds of them can often be seen cutting through the water.
St Anne's Church, dedicated to the mother of the Virgin Mary, is one of the most famous places of Christian pilgrimage on the island. Today, most of the people living in Kalpitiya at the end of the peninsula are Muslims but *Fort Calpentyn*, which was built in 1676, and the dilapidated *St Peter's Kerk*, recalls the long Dutch presence. Accommodation is not particularly cheap but very comfortable, one such example

LOW BUDGET

▶ On Saturday and Sunday, the southern side of Viharamahadevi Park, along Coomaraswamy Mawatha in Colombo, turns into Sri Lanka's longest gallery with wonderful (and inexpensive) paintings. This is where the local art scene displays their creations.

▶ The *Food Court* in the basement of the *Crescat Boulevard (75 Galle Road | Colombo)* shopping centre has a wide choice of very reasonably priced dishes.

▶ The *Parisare (97/1 Rosmead Place | tel. 011 2 69 47 49)* in Colombo's upper-class Cinnamon Gardens district rents three comfortable, reasonably priced rooms in a private house.

Negombo: in the afternoon the fishing boats return to the shore

is the Makara Resorts – Dolphin Beach *(Alankuda, Ettalai | tel. 077 7 72 32 72 | www.dolphinbeach.lk)* , with spacious air-conditioned luxurious tents in Indian Rajasthan style with a personalised butler service and an interesting programme of excursions.

KUMUDU VALLEY (132 A5) *(⌀ B12)*

This is the name of the hotspot for all manner of water sports on the island; the best time is in winter from November in April. Holger Brümmer runs a training camp for water-skiing, kite-surfing and – first and foremost – INSIDER TIP wakeboarding *(www.wakeboardcamps.com)* at the mouth of the Ging Oya River near Kochchikade, 5km (3mi) north of Negombo. Wake-boarding is a trendy new water sport using a board pulled by a boat; it combines the actions of water-skiing, surfing and snowboarding. The atmosphere is young and laid-back and the participants either live in the *Kumudu Valley Resort (10 extremely well equipped chalets | Thaldeka Road, Naimadana | tel. 031 22 52 27 | www.*

kumuduvalley.com | Moderate) or in more reasonably priced hotels and guesthouses in the vicinity.

INSIDER TIP MARAWILA
(132 A5) *(⌀ B12)*

The small village on the coast, around 20km (12mi) north of Negombo, is famous for its batik products. The well-known Budhi firm has its headquarters in the village. Mainly package-deal tourists spend their all inclusive holidays here or in Waikkal, which is somewhat closer to Negombo, in the two mid–range hotels, the *Dolphin (148 rooms | Kammal South, Waikkal | tel. 031 2 27 77 88 | www.serendibleisure.com | Moderate)* and *Ranweli Holiday Village (84 rooms | Waikkal | tel. 031 2 27 73 59 | www.ranweli.com | Moderate)* and other houses. The region between Waikkal and Marawila has preserved much of its traditional charm and the long beaches are unspoilt while the tropical green hinterland delights visitors with its many canals, lagoons and endless groves of coconut palms.

THE SOUTH

This is the most-visited beach region – a tropical coastline with beautiful bays – and there are no skyscrapers to spoil the view. The beaches are only interrupted by a few old colonial towns that are well worth visiting.

The old town of Galle, which was fortified by the Dutch, is the most beautiful of these. The villages of Beruwala, Alutgama and Bentota, with their shops, tailors, bars and hotels, have almost become a single settlement. The operators of the large hotels and owners of the small guesthouses and restaurants between Kalutara and Galle have done all they can to reconstruct their houses following the damage caused by the tsunami. Hikkaduwa and Unawatuna, with plenty of budget accommodation, are Sri Lanka's top beach locations for party-goers while the secluded bays and beaches east of Matara – and, especially in Mirissa – attract holidaymakers looking for peace and quiet.

BENTOTA/ BERUWALA

(136 B3–4) (*Ш C16*) A long band of palm trees and beach extends 60km (37mi) to the south of Colombo. This is the site

Fairytale beaches and a lush, green hinterland – nature lovers will be delighted with what Sri Lanka's south has to offer

of Sri Lanka's most famous seaside resorts of Beruwala and Bentota, with small Alutgama in between.

The narrow coastal strip between the Bento River and the sea started to be developed for beach tourism in the 1970s and this is where the greatest concentration of hotels and guesthouses can be found. Water sports' enthusiasts will certainly be happy here: the reefs off the coast are ideal for snorkelling and the wide, muddy river is perfect for boat trips into the hinterland. The deeper one travels inland, the more romantic the atmosphere of the jungle becomes. It is particularly peaceful if you avoid the boats with loud, smelly outboard motors rather glide through the tropical idyll on an outrigger boat. The best time is in the early hours of the morning when the

The Kachchimalai mosque in Beruwala: the oldest on the island

KACHCHIMALAI MOSQUE ☙

The oldest Islamic place of worship in Sri Lanka is located on a promontory near Beruwala. The terrace has a fantastic panoramic view of one of the many picturesque bays of the southwest coast. The mosque was probably built in the 13th century although Arab merchants already settled in the area in the 1st century. Beruwala has maintained its traditionally Muslim character to this day. *Daily 8am–6pm*

river is to be a real paradise full of birdlife. But beware: the sea can be rather tricky along this section of the coast. At some places, the tides create dangerous undercurrents (not only in the monsoon season) so heed the local warnings.

SIGHTSEEING

FISH MARKET IN BERUWALA

Every morning a fascinating – but bloody – spectacle takes place at the harbour next to the old mosque. The catch of barracudas and swordfish, sharks and tuna fish – and unfortunately sometimes even small whales – is cut into pieces on the sand. `INSIDER TIP` A boat trip to the lighthouse perched on a rock off the coast is a considerably gentler affair. The trip only costs a few rupees and just takes a couple of minutes but you will be rewarded with a spectacular view from the ☙ top of the tower and be able to take some lovely photographs of the mosque, harbour and the coast fringed with palms.

FOOD & DRINK WHERE TO STAY

There are many small restaurants along the busy A2 highway between Beruwala and Indurawa south of Bentota. The *Golden Grill* in Bentota (at the National Holiday Resort) is one of the tried and tested establishments popular with holidaymakers from the beach hotels. As a rule, the owners of the privately-run hotels also offer good food at reasonable prices and they are also open to non-guests. They have the best contacts to the local fishermen and buy fish straight from the nets: the establishments include the *Hemadan,* the *Sunil Lanka* and the *Terrena* where the Austrian proprietor also brings a touch of his homeland to his cooking and serves meals in a pleasant environment *(all Budget).*

AIDA (AYURVEDA)

This extremely beautiful, spacious resort on the Bento River enjoys an excellent reputation. This applies equally to the atmosphere, doctors and treatments offered. A large garden with a swimming pool is also part of the complex *(12 A Mangoda Mawatha | tel. 034 2 27 11 37 | www.aidaayurveda.com | Moderate–Expensive).* The *Aida 2 (tel. 034 2 2718 88 | Moderate–Expensive)* in *Indurawa,* a ten minute drive away, is much smaller and more intimate. The disadvantage with Aida 2 is that it is on Galle Road, which makes it rather noisy.

AYUBOWAN SWISS LANKA

This complex in the southern part of Bentota is only a few hundred feet away from the beach, making it ideal for families. The swimming pool in the tropical garden and the six rooms (varying standards) make it a good choice for any budget. *171 Galle Road | tel. 034 2 27 59 13 | www.ayubowan. ch/default_e.html | Budget–Moderate*

HEMADAN

Friendly guesthouse in the Alutgama district is right on the Bento River and serves the best lobster and jumbo prawns in the area. The owner Hemasiri will be happy to provide information on where to go and how to organise a river trip. *10 rooms | 25 A River Avenue | tel. 034 227 53 20 | www. hemadan.dk | Budget*

LANKA PRINCESS

Large, four-storey, German-run beach hotel in Beruwala. Many package holidaymakers had their first contact with Ayurveda here and subsequently returned for further treatments. Ayurveda guests have their own private restaurant. *110 rooms | tel. 034 2 27 67 11 | www.lanka princess.com | Expensive*

INSIDERTIP SINGHARAJA BAKERY & RESTAURANT

The best bakery on the west coast sells delicious, fresh bread and rolls on the ground floor and there is a clean buffet restaurant on the first. *120 Galle Road | Budget–Moderate*

VIVANTA BY TAJ – BENTOTA

This is probably the most pleasant of all the deluxe hotels on the southwest coast. It lies slightly above one of the longest beaches on the island and has a large garden and many amenities. As with most of the other beach hotels in the area, you will hear the train rattling by in the background several times a day but the sound will certainly not disturb you. *162 rooms | tel. 034 5 55 55 55 | www.vivantabytaj.com | Expensive*

SPORTS & ACTIVITIES

BENTOTA CLUB

This well-known resort's website lists Bentota as the 'water sports capital of Sri Lanka'. The complex stretches along a peninsula between the Bentota River and Indian Ocean and offers a wide range of sporting activities – also for those who are not staying at the resort. *Paradise Island, Alutgama | tel. 034 2 27 51 67 | www.clubbentota.com*

SUNSHINE WATERSPORTS

Thusal Gunawardena and his young team offer just about everything holidaymakers like to do on and under the water – jet-skiing, wake-boarding, banana boat rides,

---

MARCO POLO HIGHLIGHTS

⭐ **Brief Garden**
A magnificent, green oasis
→ p. 50

⭐ **Old town in Galle**
A living open-air museum that is a testimony of the colonial era → p. 50

⭐ **Mirissa**
Inexpensive accommodation and pleasant pubs on a perfect beach → p. 52

⭐ **Yala West National Park**
Track down elephants, buffalos, monitor lizards and birds → p. 54

deep-sea and river fishing, as well as diving and surfing courses. Thusal knows the region like the back of his hand and has lots of helpful tips and information. *River Avenue, Alutgama | tel. 034 4 28 93 79 | www.sunshinewatersports.net*

WHERE TO GO

AHUNGALLA (136 B4) *(M C17)*

This long, picture-perfect beach is around 15km (9mi) south of Bentota. There are no high-rise buildings looming between the palms making it the most beautiful stretch of coast between Bentota and Galle. However, if you decide to go for a long stroll along the beach, be prepared for all the annoying touts, self-appointed tour guides and 'donation collectors'. The *Lotus Villa (14 rooms | 162/19 Wathuregama, Ahungalla | tel. 091 2 26 40 82 | www.lotus-villa.com | Moderate)*, is one of the best Ayurveda resorts on the coast and offers Panchakarma treatments lasting at least two weeks.

AMBALANGODA (136 B5) *(M C17)*

A lively bazaar, a Dutch era church and wooden fishing boats make Ambalangoda (22km/14mi south of Bentota) a pleasant excursion destination. Ambalangoda is famous for its mask carvers and the family business with the longest tradition is *Ariyapala & Sons (426 Patabendimulla)*, they also have a *Mask Museum (daily 8am–6pm | free admission)* that is well worth a visit.

BRIEF GARDEN ★ ● (136 B4) *(M C16)*

The enchanted park 10km (6mi) northeast of Bentota was the estate of the eccentric hedonist and artist Bevis Bawa, who died in 1992. This trip to paradise will not only be a delight for lovers of things botanical. The path starting in the Alutgama section of town leads to the east through the Muslim village of Dharga and further through rubber plantations. *Daily 9am–5pm | entrance fee 1000 SLRs*

KALUTARA (136 B3) *(M C15)*

A *dagoba*, which is part of the *Gangatilaka Vihara* temple complex, towers up over the city (pop. 110,000) 31km (19mi) to the north of Bentota. If they are Buddhists, the local drivers all stop here to make an offering. They throw a few small coins into a box and sometimes lay flowers in front of one of the many statues of Buddha under the banyan trees on the other side of the street, opposite the large dagoba. That is supposed to ensure safe travel and a happy homecoming. The locals also appreciate it when tourists follow this custom.

GALLE

(132 C6) *(M D18)* Sri Lanka's best preserved old town dates from the Dutch period (17th/18th century) and feels like a living open-air museum, the walled town lies in front of a large modern city (pop. 120,000).

The Fort has become very popular in recent years and an increasing number of well-heeled foreigners have settled there. New boutiques and cafés have sprung up and old houses have been converted into exclusive hotels. The New Oriental Hotel that opened in 1865 has been renamed the Amangalla and is now one of the best hotels on the southern coast.

SIGHTSEEING

OLD TOWN IN GALLE ★

To get general overview take a stroll once around the old fort district on the grass-covered ramparts of the old fortress, past the Moon, Star, Aeolus, Clippenberg, Neptune, Triton, Utrecht, Aurora, Akerslot,

Zwart and Sun bastions (walk anticlockwise from the New Gate), the lighthouse and former New Oriental Hotel. The origins of the fort can be traced back to the 16th century when the Portuguese built a small fortress on this rock (Singhalese: *gala*). They changed *gala* into the new name of the town *Gallo* (Portuguese for rooster). The bird still adorns the town's coat of arms, clearly visible on the inner side of the Old Gate. From 1640 to 1796 the new colonial power, the Dutch, left their mark by expanding the fortress and building churches. Worth a visit is the *Groote Kerk*. Originally Reformed, later Presbyterian and then Anglican – the church was founded by the wife of the Dutch commander of the fortress in 1754. Walk from the lighthouse past the large mosque (a former church) along *Leyn Baan*, *Church Street* and *Church Cross*. The Pettah, as the colourful bazaar district is also called here, lies outside of the fort opposite the cricket stadium in the new part of town.

HISTORICAL MANOR HOUSE

The Muslim merchant Gaffar has collected many objects that once belonged to a Dutch household. There is also an art gallery and a charming inner courtyard. *Daily 9am–6pm | free admission | 31–39 Leyn Baan Street*

You will find traces of colonial rule everywhere in Galle's old town

---

FOOD & DRINK

Within the fort there are a growing number of pleasant cafés and restaurants while hotels steeped in history such as *Fort Printers* on Pedlar Street or the *Galle Fort Hotel* on Church Street are also inviting places to stop for a break.

PEDLAR'S INN CAFÉ

The café in the old colonial post office is open from morning to evening and serves good breakfasts, delicious coffee and cakes, and dinner. *92 Pedlar Street | www.pedlarsinn.com | Budget*

SERENDIPITY ARTS CAFÉ ●

Whether you decide to sit at the long communal table in the room with funky pictures and graffiti on the walls, or on the first floor balcony , the atmosphere is great, the food quite good and the books on the shelves provide plenty of reading material. *56 Leyn Baan Street | Budget*

SHOPPING

Street vendors in the Fort District sell lace tablecloths and carvings and there are also some pretty shops in the small streets. Some gemstone dealers work together with artistic craftsmen and *A. R. M. Cassim (57 Leyn Baan Street)* has some lovely old pieces.

A dream destination: the beach at Mirissa

WHERE TO STAY

INSIDER TIP CLOSENBERG ⚓

The harbour master Captain Bailey's former home high above Galle Bay 3km (2mi) to the east of Galle Fort has been a hotel since the beginning of the 20th century. A good place for sundowners and a stylish dinner. *21 rooms | 11 Closenburg Road | tel. 0912 23 22 41 | www.closenburg hotel.com | Moderate*

DUTCH HOUSE/SUN HOUSE

Those who can afford to stay in one of the expensive suites in the Dutch House (Doomberg) dating back to 1712, will appreciate the atmosphere just as much as those in the Sun House (opposite), built by a Scottish spice merchant in 1860. No traffic noise penetrates this luxurious idyll; mealtimes are taken on a terrace that flows into the garden. This is as exquisite as it gets. *18 Upper Dickson Road | tel. 0914 38 02 75 | www.thesunhouse.com | Expensive*

JETWING LIGHTHOUSE

One of the most comfortable coastal hotels on the island, with a dreamlike beach in front of the large garden 3km (2mi) west of Galle. The house has been decorated in a style reminiscent of Dutch colonial buildings. *60 rooms | Dadella | tel. 0912 22 37 44 | www.jetwinghotels.com | Expensive*

WHERE TO GO

MIRISSA ★ (137 D6) (⑰ E18)

The name itself conjures up the image of a fairytale beach. The small bay is the favourite destination of a great number of travellers including many surfers. The *Palace Mirissa (Coparamulla | tel. 0412 25 13 03 | www.palacemirissa.com | Moderate)* stands out among all the accommodation offered here: nine cabanas on a cliff between coconut palms and frangipani trees. **INSIDER TIP** A trip from Mirissa into the interior will be rewarded with many delightful experiences. Hire a bicycle and pedal around authentic villages such as *Denipitiya* or along the banks of the Polwatta River where the landscape alternates between lush vegetation and rubber plantations. *30km (19mi) west of Galle*

UNAWATUNA (136 C6) (⑰ D18)

The 2km (1mi) long crescent-shaped bay just a mile or so from Galle – and its cheaper accommodation – have made Unawatuna especially popular with independent tourists. Snorkelers will also enjoy the wealth of marine life on the reef off the coast and experienced wreck divers will be able to explore the **INSIDER TIP** sailing ship, the 'Rangoon', that found its final resting place 30m (100ft) under the surface of the water in 1863. There are several diving schools on the beach including the acclaimed *Seahorse Divers,* the *Submarine Diving School* and the *Unawatuna Diving Centre.* **INSIDER TIP** *Sun N Sea (10 rooms | 324 Matara Road, Ganahena | tel. 091 2 28 32 00 | www.sunnsea.net | Moderate)*, a hotel wedged in between the main road and the beach at Unawatuna, is particularly recommended not only for its lovely location – right on the seaside – and its stylish rooms but also for their delicious meals. The seafood dishes alone are enough to gladden any gourmet's heart and the rice and curry are also delicious. To a large extent, the house still breathes the spirit of Muharam Perera, the woman who established the hotel, and died in 2006. ﾐ *Thambapanni Retreat (11 rooms, 2 suites | Yakdehimulla Road | tel. 091 2 23 45 88 | www.thambapanni.biz | Budget–Moderate)* is not at the beach but is located in a wonderfully peaceful site on Rumassala Hill. Beautifully decorated rooms with spectacular views of the sea or jungle.

WELIGAMA (137 D6) (𝄞 E18)

Here, between Ahangama and Weligama (pop. 60,000, barely 30km/19mi from Galle), is the only place where fishermen perform their work sitting on stilts in the ocean. They are shown on postcards, book covers and and are happy to pose for anybody who wants to take a photograph – for a tip. The *Ahangama Easy Beach (Colombo-Matara Road, KM 136 | tel. 091 2 28 20 28 | www.easybeach.info | Budget)*, with its eight rooms, two cabanas and a large garden, is a wonderful place for surfers (surfboard rental) and families to stay. Sonila and Maithri Gunaratna opened their small, luxurious hideaway *South Point (Kathaluwa district | mobile tel. 077 3 03 94 04 | www.southpointvilla.com | Expensive)* near Ahangama, 6km (4mi) west of Weligama, in December 2004 a mere two weeks before the tsunami catastrophe. They were lucky and very little any damage was done to their incredibly beautiful property. The villa with a pool has only three rooms all well equipped and furnished with exquisite taste.

HAMBANTOTA

(138 B6) (𝄞 J17) This mainly Muslim town (pop. 70,000, 110km/68mi from Galle), has little of interest for tourists, except the beaches in the surrounding areas, but it is now being developed – with an international airport and a deep water port – into the economic centre of the chronically poor southeast.

There is a colourful spectacle on the beach every day: in the morning and evening, the fishermen work on their boats, unload their catch and bring in their nets. There are many evaporation basins for the production of sea salt in the dry environment.

SIGHTSEEING

BUNDALA NATIONAL PARK

The 9138 acre reserve (18km/11mi east of Hambantota) stretches along the coast and consists of lagoons, sand dunes and bushes. With 139 indigenous and 58 species of migratory birds, including pink flamingos, it is a paradise for ornithologists. Four species of turtles lay their eggs on the beach. *Entrance fee US$10 plus*

LOW BUDGET

▶ The *Ocean View Guest House* is located in Fort Galle. Pleasant rooftop garden with sea view. *6 rooms | 80 Light House Street | tel. 091 2 24 27 17 | www.oceanviewlk.biz*

▶ The traditional *Cool Spot* in Hikkaduwa serves tasty seafood dishes and its reasonable prices make it a popular meeting place for travellers on a budget. *327 Galle Road*

additional charges and taxes. Jeeps are the only vehicles permitted in the park (half-day tours: 5000–7000 SLRs)

FOOD & DRINK

JADE GREEN RESTAURANT

This restaurant's open-view kitchen celebrates the great variety of Asian cuisine. Good seafood at reasonable prices. *Tissa Road | tel. 047 2 22 06 92 | Budget*

WHERE TO STAY

OASIS AYURVEDA BEACH RESORT

The resort lies in a secluded location in a large garden 7km (4mi) to the west of Hambantota. It unites traditional Ayurvedic treatments with a level of hotel comfort that will satisfy the most demanding guests. *40 rooms in the main house, 10 bungalows | Sisilasagama | tel. 047 2 22 06 50 | www.oasis-ayurveda.com | Moderate*

WHERE TO GO

KATARAGAMA (138 C4) *(ɰ K16)*

It is only worth spending some time here almost 180km (112mi) away from Galle once a year: at the time of the Esala full moon (July/August) when hundreds of thousands of people flock to the Hindu-Buddhist festival in honour of the god of war Skanda, who is also known as *Kataragama*. The main attractions are the firewalkers and the penitents who chastise themselves in a trance state, pierce their tongues or have themselves 'hung up' on hooks stuck in their flesh.

TISSAMAHARAMA (138 C5) *(ɰ J17)*

Tissamaharama is around 150km (93mi) from Galle. *Dagobas* and ruins are reminders that the south Singhalese realm of Ruhuna was once ruled from here. The largest *dagoba* rises out of the field of ruins close to the rest house at its delightful location on a lake. It was built in the 1st century BC. The freshwater reservoirs *(wewas)* in the area are a paradise for birds and birdwatchers alike.

UDA WALAWE NATIONAL PARK (137 F3–4, 138 A4) *(ɰ G16)*

This nature reserve has the largest concentration of elephants. It is a good 65km (40mi) away from Hambantota, towards the highlands. The 119mi² national park has a gigantic reservoir at its centre and is home to an estimated 700 elephants as well as swamp crocodiles, sambar deer and many varieties of water birds. The best time to visit the park is early in the morning or late in the afternoon. The *Elephant Transit Home*, around 5km (3mi) from the entrance to the park, was founded in 1995 and today provides shelter for orphaned elephants. *Entrance fee US$15 plus additional charges and taxes*

YALA WEST NATIONAL PARK ★ (139 D–E 3–4) *(ɰ K–L16)*

The large reserve is characterised by a thorn bush savannah, numerous lakes and brackish water. It is usually best to go on a game drive in the afternoon rather than in the morning. The drivers and rangers usually spot the wildlife – crocodiles, monitor lizards, mongoose and wild boar – long before the guests. Elephants will almost certainly cross your path but the shy leopards are very adept at hiding themselves in the thickets. Peacocks, pelicans, storks and a great number of colourful little birds are also on the programme but the price for it is rather high: *entrance fee US$15 plus additional charges and taxes and the cost for the off-road vehicle (4000–7000 SLRs). Contact: Independent Safari Jeep Association (ISJA) | 2 Punchi Akurugoda | Tissamaharama | tel. 047 5 67 14 80 | www.yalajeepsafari.com*

You are almost guaranteed to see elephants in the Yala National Park

HIKKADUWA

(136 B5) *(🛅 C17)* **Once known as Hippie-Duwa this small town then become synonymous with mass tourism on Sri Lanka and is now a meeting place for active travellers who spend their days in the water and their nights in one of the many beach bars.**

The colourful Sunday market, which emerged from Hikkaduwa's alternative days, offers a lot of art along with plenty of tat. There is a variety of water sports (diving and surfing) and well as trips in a glass-bottom boat. However, the many beach boys are annoying – don't fall for their advances!

FOOD & DRINK

MOON BEAM
Right on the beach, next to the hotel of the same name; especially good for lovers of seafood. Shelton, the host, always makes sure that his guests have plenty of fun. *568 Galle Road | Budget–Moderate*

ENTERTAINMENT

TOP SECRET
The perfect place to start a night in the tropics. The music is not too loud, you can feel the sand under your feet and just relax and enjoy yourself (*Galle Road | Naragama District*). On Friday, the crowd moves on to *Vibration (495 Galle Road)*, and on Saturday things really get moving at *Mambo's* on the beach.

WHERE TO STAY

AMAYA REEF
Hikkaduwa's number one hotel with very spacious, tastefully decorated rooms on only two floors. *43 rooms | 400 Galle Road | tel. 091 4 38 32 44 | www.amayaresorts. com | Moderate*

THE HARMONY GUESTHOUSE
A popular place for travellers, in a great location right on the beach; 13 modest but clean rooms. *698 Galle Road | Narigama District | tel. 091 22 77 55 | www. srilanka-holiday.info | Budget*

LAWRENCE HILL PARADISE

The bungalows with a total of 14 large rooms are spread throughout a lush garden. A lovely swimming pool, the peaceful location (a five minute walk from town and the sea) and – above all – the welcoming atmosphere may mean that you won't even feel the need to go to the beach. The hotel is only open to guests taking Ayurveda spa treatments. *47 Waulagoda Middle Road | tel. 091 2 27 75 44 | Moderate*

WHERE TO GO

DODANDUWA (136 C5) (⌀ D17–18)

The small village around 5km (3mi) southwest of Hikkaduwa and the ● Rathgama Lagoon with its wealth of birdlife is perfect for boat tours *(from Eco Village | ca. 400 SLRs per person)*. The delicate colours at sunrise and sunset make a trip particularly beautiful. Monks lead a life of seclusion and meditation on *Hermitage Island (not open to the public)*. The ● *House of Lotus (7 rooms | 175 Galle Road | tel. 091 2 26 72 46 | www.house-of-lotus.com | Moderate)*, with its colonial ambience offers an ideal holiday for both body and soul. A balanced diet, yoga and meditation courses are all available and the beach is not far away.

MATARA

(137 E6) (⌀ F18) This lively trading city (pop. 80,000, 45km/28mi east of Galle) has been the Colombo line railway terminus since 1895.

Its location at the mouth of the Nilwala River made Sri Lanka's southernmost city important hub for the lucrative cinnamon trade under the Portuguese and Dutch. It developed into an important educational centre when the University of Ruhuna, designed by the renowned architect Geoffrey Bawa, was opened in 1984.

SIGHTSEEING

The old Dutch *fort* with its clock tower and the smaller *Star Fortress* built in 1765 are two of the city's attractions. The snow-white *Muhiyideen Jumma Mosque* rises up directly on the river and there is a lovely beach in Polhena, 3km (2mi) west of the city. An octagonal lighthouse in Dondra, 6km (4mi) away, has marked the most southerly point in Sri Lanka since 1889. The *Devi Nuwara Temple* there, with the blue shrine in honour of Vishnu, is the site of the ten-day *Dondra Perahera* every year in July/August.

FOOD & DRINK

MAYURA BEACH RESORT

The restaurant on the ground floor of the hotel serves decent curries. *33 Beach Road | tel. 041 2 22 32 74 | Budget*

WHERE TO STAY

The fabulous beaches in the surroundings make it a good idea to travel a bit further eastwards along the coast where there are some very beautiful seaside accommodation options on the stretch to Dikwella *(24km/15 mi)*.

TALALLA RETREAT

Guests will find all the creature comforts they need in the two-storey villas set in the midst of a tropical garden, complete with pool, and right on the beach around 15km (9mi) east of Matara. The establishment offers services ranging from yoga courses and massages to surfing retreats. *32 rooms | Sampaya House, Talalla Gandara | tel. 041 2 25 91 71 | www.talalla retreat.com | Moderate*

WHERE TO GO

MULKIRIGALA (137 F5) (*⑪ G17*)

One of the oldest monasteries in the south of the island is centred on a rocky rise near Mulkirigala, 55km (34mi) north-east of Matara: the *Pahala Vihara*. It is believed that Buddhist hermits settled here as early as the 2nd century BC. The various monastery buildings have been

It is quite likely that you will discover a picture-perfect, secluded bay without any kiosks and beach boys. Sea turtles lay their eggs at one of the loveliest in Rekawa, 50km (31mi) east of Matara. Tourists can watch the **INSIDER TIP** nocturnal events under the supervision of the *Turtle Conservation Project (TCP)* (dark clothing, no flash photography!). *Information and bookings: tel. 077 790 29 15 (Mr.*

The lighthouse in Dondra watches over the southernmost point of the island

built on and around the mountain and you will have to climb up 450 steps to get to the stupa at the top and admire the spectacular panoramic view of the countryside. *Daily 6am–6pm | entrance fee 200 SLRs*

REKAWA (137 E–F6) (*⑪ F–G18*)

Those in the know enjoy the peaceful beaches between Matara and Tangalla. Just take any one of the side roads leading off of the main road towards the beach.

Saman) or 077 781 05 09 (Mr. Thushan) | 1000 SLRs

WEWURUKANNALA (137 F6) (*⑪ F18*)

The 50m (164ft) high statue of Buddha near *Wewurukannala Vihara* around 2km (1mi) north of Dikwella is the largest in Sri Lanka. A ten-storey building painted with scenes from the life of Buddha leading into the head of the figure is also part of the complex, which was built in the early 1970s. *During the day | free admission*

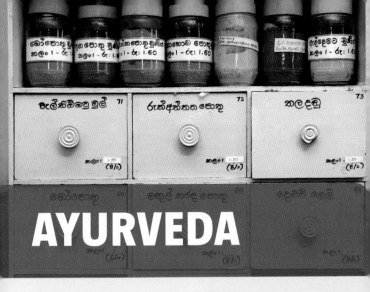

AYURVEDA

On Sri Lanka, the ancient 'knowledge (veda) of a long, healthy life (ayur)' has developed into a new type of wellness holiday and the offers range from beach resort spas to specialised health clinics. During a Ayurvedic massage, the therapist spreads warmed oil over the back of the guest while they lie on a bench made with the wood of the neem tree. The hotel offers everything from flower and herbal steam baths to beauty treatments and a variety of massages.

Panchakarma therapy, which usually lasts for two weeks, is very different from these kinds of treatments and is offered by specialised Ayurvedic resorts with the aim of purifying and detoxing the body. An Ayurveda doctor first makes a pulse and tongue diagnosis and a consultation to determine the state of the patient's constitution. He then builds an individual treatment plan with herbs, oils, baths and massages. Successes range from a strengthened immune system to improvements in skin diseases, rheumatism, high blood pressure, joint pains and weight problems. It is also suitable for treating tinnitus and for cancer aftercare.

A PART OF THE COSMOS

Two writings from the 1st/2nd century form the theoretical basis for Ayurveda: 'Caraka Samhita', a description of the human body, and the 'Sushruta Samhita', a textbook on surgery. The human being is seen as part of the cosmos and is also constituted of the cosmic base elements: ether, air, fire, water and earth. These five elements, in the form of three organic streams or vital forces – the *doshas* – are responsible for the body, spirit and soul being in balance. The *doshas* have various functions and they are individually weighted in each person: the *Vata Dosha* controls movement, the organs of the senses and the nervous system; the *Pitta Dosha* is responsible for the metabolism, digestion and emotions; the *Kapha Dosha* is concerned with the body structure and its defence, and spiritual equilibrium. If the *Doshas* are balanced, the person is healthy and illness will only result when things are out of balance. Ayurveda treatment therefore aims at bringing the body, spirit and soul back into a balanced state.

Wellness or health cure – bring your body, spirit and soul back into balance with a variety of Ayurveda treatments

PRACTICAL ADVICE

It is absolutely essential to be well prepared for any Ayurveda treatment. If you are considering treatment you can also opt for a specialised tour operator that offers an all inclusive tour. Most of the doctors in Sri Lank speak English. You will find specialised clinics and hotels with Ayurveda spas mentioned in the individual regional chapters of this guide.

AUSTRIAN BEACH RESORT
Boutique hotel on the south coast that offers a combination of wellness, beach holiday and Ayurvedic treatment. *10 rooms | Kemagoda, Dickwella | tel. 041 2 25 67 26 | www.austrianbeach.com | Moderate*

HERITANCE AYURVEDA MAHA GEDARA
This beach resort in minimalist design with 24 treatment rooms offers forms of therapy to help its guests learn how to practice a healthy lifestyle. *64 rooms | Beruwala | tel. 034 5 55 50 00 | www.heritancehotels.com | Moderate–Expensive*

JETWING AYURVEDA PAVILIONS
A stylish resort – with only twelve spacious bungalows and a special area for treatments – that places great value on giving its guests personalised care. *Ethukale, Negombo | tel. 031 2 27 67 19 | www.jetwinghotels.com | Expensive*

THILANKA
Nestled up against a mountain slope not far from a lake, this hotel has its own Ayurveda centre with a wide choice of wellness treatments. *87 rooms | 3 Sangamitta Mawatha, Kandy | tel. 081 4 47 52 00 | www.thilankahotel.com | Moderate*

THE HIGHLANDS

Explore the last Singhalese royal city, the tea country and the wild, romantic mountain landscape south of Nuwara Eliya in a three or four day excursion.

The religious sites will be the centre of your interest in Kandy. As you go further to the east, you will be fascinated by the green carpet that covers much of the hilly countryside – this is where the world's best tea grows – and the dramatically beautiful highlands around *Sri Pada* (Adam's Peak) and the unique landscape of the Horton Plains. Once you reach the old colonial summer resort of Nuwara Eliya, you will be able to immerse yourself in the bygone days of the empire.

ELLA

(138 B2) *(⫿ H14)* ⚹ **Ella may only be a small village but its views – far into the south – are more spectacular than in any other town.**

At an altitude of 1000m (3280ft) Ella offers a good selection of budget accommodation and there are excellent possibilities for hikes, including routes to *Little Adam's Peak* southeast of the village or to the 1350m (4430ft) high *Ella Rock* (some guesthouses can provide 'homemade' maps). The *Rawana Ella Cave*, around 1.5km (1mi) to the south, is not particularly interesting

Photo: Tea crop in the highlands

Between Adam's Peak and the Temple of the Tooth — wonders of nature, colonial nostalgia and Sri Lanka's religious centre

but the 100m (328ft) *Rawana Ella Falls*, about 6km (4mi) to the southeast on the road to Wellawaya, are impressive.

FOOD & DRINK
WHERE TO STAY

AMBIENTE ☆
Even if it is just to admire the panorama, this comfortable guesthouse with only eight rooms, is one of the top addresses in Ella. It is best to book well in advance as they are frequently full. *Kitalella Road | tel. 057 2 22 88 67 | www.ambiente.lk | Budget*

INSIDER TIP ZION VIEW GUEST HOUSE ☆
Gorgeous views, tastefully decorated rooms with hammocks on the terrace, delicious food and the owner's friendly

Carved out of the rock: the Buddha statue in Buduruwagala

family, who provide a wealth of tips for excursions, all mean that guests often stay longer than they originally planned. *7 rooms | Wemulla Hena | tel. 057 2 22 87 99 | www.ella-guesthouse-srilanka.com | Budget–Moderate*

SPORTS & ACTIVITIES

INSIDER TIP COOKERY COURSE
Ella Spice Garden offers a three-hour cookery course, including a communal meal, twice a day at 10.30am and 5.30pm. Advance booking is essential! *Contact: Lizzie Villa Guest House | 200 yds off Main Street | tel. 075 2 36 36 36 | 2000 SLRs*

WHERE TO GO

INSIDER TIP BADULLA (138 B1) *(∅ H14)*
The capital city (pop. 53,000) of the tea province of Uva is both the starting point and final destination of a beautiful train ride through the mountains. The city is about 50km (31mi) east of Nuwara Eliya. A Hindu temple *(Kataragama),* an English church *(St Mark's),* and, above all, a Buddhist temple *(Mutiyangana)* all make a leisurely stroll through the town worthwhile. Hikers will be attracted to the 2000m (6600ft) high *Namunukulla* that is an easy climb. Other destinations for excursions include the nearby (5km/3mi away) *Dunhinda Waterfalls,* which plunge almost 60m (200ft) into the deep, and the 300-year-old, scenically located, Bogoda Bridge (15km/9mi to the southwest).

BANDARAWELA (138 B2) *(∅ H14)*
A lively town with a pleasant atmosphere, and the most colourful markets and bazaars in the highlands. The 50km (31mi) route from Nuwara Eliya (via the B 810) passes through a beautiful landscape of rice terraces. The 300-year-old *Dowa Cave*

Temple, with a 4m(13ft) high figure of Buddha carved out of the rock, is definitely worth making a detour to see (5km/3mi to the north). The colonial-style Bandarawela *(36 small rooms | 14 Welimada Road | el. 057 2 22 25 01 | Moderate)* is a pleasant, albeit somewhat confusingly laid out, hotel.

BUDURUWAGALA (138 B3) *(ⓜ H15)*

On your way from Ella to the south coast, make a slight detour to see the rock reliefs in Buduruwagala. They can be found about 10km (6mi) southwest of Wellawaya (29km/18mi south of Ella) close to a reservoir. An almost 17m (56ft) high statue of Buddha standing upright and groups of three Bodhisattvas (to his left and right) where hewn from the rock between the 7th and 10th centuries *(daily 8am–5pm | entrance fee 200 SLRs).*

MALIGAWILA (138 C3) *(ⓜ J15)*

Not many tourists make their way to the INSIDER TIP *Buddha statue in Maligawila,* 15km (9mi) east of the village of Buttala (located between Wellawaya and Monoragala). The 7th century Buddha was erected in this ancient place of worship in 1991 after lying shattered in the jungle for centuries. Very charming atmosphere and many pilgrims from the neighbouring villages.

KANDY

MAP INSIDE BACK COVER
(133 E5) *(ⓜ F12)* **The first impression: the traffic in Kandy (pop. 150,000) is absolutely chaotic, it is noisy and you could cut the air with a knife. Can this possibly be the most beautiful town on the island?**
The second impression: with a view (from the a lookout point in Wace Park) across

WHERE TO START?
Queens Hotel: take a three-wheeler (agree on the price before you set out!) to the Queens Hotel. From there, it is only a few steps to the Temple of the Tooth. The historical colonial hotel is also extremely well located for a shopping spree along busy Dalada Veediya. The so-called Milk Lake, a pleasant place to go for a stroll, is another attraction in the immediate vicinity.

the lake to the world-famous Temple of the Tooth, the most venerated shrine for Singhalese Buddhists, to the green hills that surround the city with a gigantic statue of Buddha towering up out of them – it

MARCO POLO HIGHLIGHTS

★ **Dalada Maligawa (Temple of the Tooth)**
This is where Sri Lanka's most precious relic is kept → p. 64

★ **Aluvihara**
Monks once engraved sacred texts into palm leaves in this beautiful rock monastery → p. 69

★ **Hill Club**
Stylish dining by candlelight → p. 70

★ **Adam's Peak**
A footprint in the rock draws pilgrims; join them in a night ascent – an unforgettable experience → p. 71

★ **Horton Plains**
A hike on the high plateau finishes at Land's End → p. 72

is really a wonderful place. Kandy suffers from the problems of our times – the streets were built for oxcarts and rickshaws – but the city on five hills (in Singhalese *Kanda uda pas rata* – the British turned that into *Kandy*) has managed to retain its charms despite some architectural blunders.

DALADA MALIGAWA (TEMPLE OF THE TOOTH) ★

This temple safeguards Sri Lanka's most precious relic – one of Buddha's eyeteeth. The Singhalese also consider the relic a symbol of their power. At first glance, it is hard to understand the importance of the building: it seems to be a melange of

Popular with the locals: a stroll around Milk Lake in Kandy

SIGHTSEEING

BAHARIVA KANDA (BUDDHA STATUE)

A dazzlingly white Buddha perches on a green hill overlooking the holy city on the west, the eye catching statue forces you to pause and reflect. The statue is almost 30m (100ft) high and was consecrated in 1993 after a construction period of 15 years (with many interruptions). A lovely path, starting at the police station next to the clock tower, leads up to the statue from busy Peradeniya Road, the walk takes about half an hour at a leisurely pace.

a palace and monastery and is of little significance in terms of art history. The building as we see it today dates from the 18th century, and the distinctive octagonal tower that makes the building so conspicuous was only added at the beginning of the 19th century. It houses a library with many ancient palm-leaf manuscripts. The temple may seem rather plain from outside but it more than makes up for this with its interior full of extravagant frescoes, magnificently decorated doors and other ornamental elements. The faithful come at all hours of the day and night to lay flowers at the tooth relic shrine on the upper floor. The flow of visitors increases dramatically three times a day when a drum roll announces the opening of the ● silver studded doorways to the holy of holies for around one hour. According to the legend, the tooth was salvaged from the ashes of the Enlightened after his death (around 489 BC). Once a year, at the time of the Esala full moon (July/August), an eleven-day festival celebrates the relic. The daily temple ceremonies begin at 5.30am, 9.30am and 6.30pm and last for about one hour. *Daily 6am–8pm | entrance fee 1000 SLRs*

INSIDER TIP ▶ KIRI MUHADA (MILK LAKE)

The artificial lake in the centre of Kandy adds charm to the city. The last Singhalese King Sri Wikrama Raja Singha had it built in 1812. He called it *Kiri Muhada,* Milk Lake, after a term from a Buddhist legend of creation. It is said that the royal mistresses had their quarters on the small island in the middle of the lake. This was later the site of a British ammunition depot. A stroll around the lake is highly recommended.

NATIONAL MUSEUM

The museum is part of the old palace (behind the temple). The exhibits include folklore items, costumes and a copy of the Kandy Convention from 1815. *Tue–Sat 9am–5pm | entrance fee 500 SLRs*

INSIDER TIP ▶ TEA MUSEUM ◁

A disused tea factory now houses exhibitions about the life and work men such as James Taylor, the first to plant a tea bush in Sri Lanka, and Sir Thomas Lipton. The documents, machines and tools recreate everyday life on the plantations in times gone by. A restaurant (budget) on the top floor offers splendid views. *Tue–Sun 8.30am–4.30pm | entrance fee 500 SLRs | www.pureceylontea.com | Hantane, 3km*

(2mi) to the south, turn towards Hindagala at the Peradenya Hospital on Hantane Road

FOOD & DRINK

HELGA'S FOLLY

A weird and quirky hotel: the lobby and restaurant are full of art, furnishings and murals – all entirely over the top. People seldom come here for the food (although it is not so bad and it is pleasant to sit on the garden terrace); most come to see the very eccentric décor – from the antlers on the gaudily coloured walls to chandeliers hanging from the ceilings. The rooms are sepulchral and rather overpriced.

LOW BUDGET

▶ Club membership for 100 SLRs a day – that is the offer made by the *Kandy Garden Club*, founded in 1878, at the eastern end of the lake on Sangaraja Mawatha. Members can play tennis and billiards or try the assortment of drinks at the bar *(daily 7am–2pm and 5pm–11pm).*

▶ The ◁ *McLeod Inn* guesthouse in Kandy *(65 A Rajaphihilla Mawatha | tel. 081 2 22 28 32 | mcleod@sltnet.lk)* offers great views and ten reasonably priced rooms.

▶ High-quality tea straight from the bush in the plantations around Nuwara Eliya, such as on the ● *Mackwoods Labookellie Estate* only 10km (6mi) away on the A 5. There, you can visit the factory and taste the tea free of charge and buy many varieties at reasonable prices. *Info: www.mackwoodstea.com*

The market in Kandy brimming with produce

QUEEN'S

The German writer Hermann Hesse stayed here in 1911. You can browse through his book 'Out of India' in the lobby or at the pool bar. A tea break or drink can also be recommended. *64 rooms | Dalada Veediya | tel. 081 2 23 30 26 and 2 22 28 13 | www.queenshotel.lk | Moderate*

SRIRAM

Kandy's best Indian serves reasonably-priced delicacies in cheerful surroundings. Don't miss out on the chicken in coconut and tomato sauce or one of the delicious vegetarian dishes on the menu. *87 Srimath Bennet Soysa Veediya (Colombo Street) | Budget*

SHOPPING

KANDY CITY CENTRE ●

The KCC houses branches of many Sri Lankan chains including *Odel*, *Hemeedia* and *Ranjanas* for fashion, *Vijitha Yapa Bookshop* for literature and *Spa Ceylon* for Ayurveda and wellness products. *Mlesna*, the best tea shop chain is also represented and sells all sorts of tea and a variety of accessories. *5 Dalada Veediya*

32 Frederick E. de Silva Mawatha | tel. 081 2 23 45 71 | www.helgasfolly.com | Expensive

INSIDER TIP SLIGHTLY CHILLED (BAMBOO GARDEN) ≋

Located on a hillock, there are some wonderful views from the terrace of this trendy restaurant. The Chinese dishes are especially tasty. *29 A Anagarika Dharmapala Mawatha | tel. 081 4 47 60 99 | Budget*

THE PUB

You can watch the world go by from the balcony and then tuck into the good pasta and meat dishes served inside. *36 Dalada Veediya | Budget*

MARKET

Don't be put off by the ugly exterior; the grey walls make the building look like a prison. Once inside, the stalls with their colourful tropical fruit and vegetables create a cheerful atmosphere. Stick to your guns when bargaining; the salespeople like to charge tourists outrageous prices.

INSIDER TIP ODEL LUV SL

The fashion retailer offers attractive Sri Lankan goods such as clothes, accessories and charming souvenirs, located at the western end of the Queens Hotel. *5 Dalada Veediya | www.odel.lk*

SELYN ☺

A women's initiative that sells high-quality fabrics and clothing in a small shop near the Temple of the Tooth. *71/1 Temple Street*

SPORTS & ACTIVITIES

KANDY DANCE

This is a traditional dance that originated in Kandy and although the performances have become rather touristy, they are still a feast for the eyes (less so for the ears). Performances are given at three locations: *Kandyan Arts Association (321 Sangaraja Mawatha), Kandy Lake Club (Sangamitta Mawatha, northeast of the lake)* and *YMBA (Rajapihilla Mawatha, southwest of the lake/ entrance fee at all places 500 SLRs / 5.30–6.30pm).*

MEDITATION

Those who are interested in meditation will find many possibilities in Sri Lanka, one such recommended venue is *Nilambe,* a scant 30km (19mi) southeast of Kandy in a magnificent mountain setting. To get there take the bus from central Kandy towards Galaha until you reach the *Nilambe Junction.* From there you can either go on foot along a steep path through a tea plantation (follow the 'Nilambe Bungalow' signs) or take a tuk-tuk up the winding road but it isn't really any quicker. You need to have a sleeping bag with you because nights in the mountains can be very cold. You should not only be prepared for the very modest accommodation (separated by gender) but also for a rigorous daily schedule: 4.30–7am walking and sitting meditation followed by tea and a simple breakfast; 8–11am meditation; midday, lunch; 2–5pm meditation and a tea break; 6–8pm meditation and singing. You need

not book in advance; you can come and go as you please. The master in Nilambe is Upul Gamage and he can sometimes be reached by telephone *(mobile 0777 80 45 55)* between 7am and 8am. For more information visit *www.nilambe.org.*

The *Buddhist Publication Society* at the eastern point of the Milk Lake *(54 Sanharaja Mawatha / tel. 081 2223679 / www.bps.lk)* or *www.buddhanet.net* is a good source of general information.

WHERE TO STAY

CINNAMON CITADEL KANDY

Formerly the Chaaya Citadel, this mid-range hotel is in a peaceful location on the Mahaweli River. Parts of the hotel complex were built at different times but come together to form a harmonious ensemble. Large garden with swimming pool. Extra tip: ask about boat trips (1–2 hours): adventurous and idyllic! *121 rooms, 5 suites / 124 Srimath Kuda Ratwatta Mawatha / tel. 081 2 23 43 65 / www.cinna monhotels.com/CinnamonCitadelKandy. htm / Moderate*

FOREST GLEN

This welcoming guesthouse, with only eight rooms, on the outskirts of the Udawattakele Nature Reserve provides the perfect accommodation for nature buffs who want to be entertained by birdsong as they eat their breakfast. *150/6 Lady Gordon's Drive / tel. 081 2 22 22 39 / www.forestglenkandy.com / Budget*

MAHAWELI REACH

The most pleasant of the large hotels in Kandy is located on the river a little out of the centre town. The rooms, balconies and pool are exceptionally large. *115 rooms / 35 P.B.A. Weerakoon Mawatha / tel. 081 4 47 27 27 / www.mahaweli.com / Moderate–Expensive*

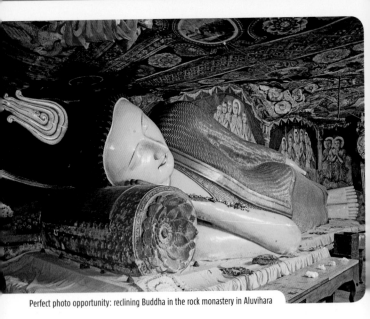

Perfect photo opportunity: reclining Buddha in the rock monastery in Aluvihara

SUISSE

A partially renovated colonial legend that has a delightful location on the south-east shore of Milk Lake, pleasant atmosphere but sometimes the service is a little slow. If you are lucky, you will be given a room with a balcony with a view over Milk Lake. *100 rooms | 30 Sangaraja Mawatha | tel. 081 2 22 26 37 | www.hotelsuisse.lk | Moderate*

INSIDER TIP ▶ VILLA ROSA

This small hotel is a hideaway for stressed souls. The location above the river, around 15 minutes by car from the Temple of the Tooth, is idyllic; the furnishings are discreet and tasteful and the garden magnificent. Tip: there is a small but excellent Ayurveda area for Panchakarma therapies and individual treatments; a competent medical management and friendly and experienced therapists. The owner is also happy to give you some great tips for excursions. *10 rooms | 71/18 Dodanwela-Passage, Asgiriya | tel. 081 2 215 55 56 | www.villarosa-kandy.com | Expensive*

INFORMATION

SRI LANKA TOURISM INFORMATION CENTRE

Kandy City Centre 5 | Dalada Vidiya | tel. 081 2 22 26 61 | excellent website: www.kandycity.org

WHERE TO GO

HUNAS FALLS (133 E–F5) (∅ F12)

Nature lovers will find a wonderful hiking area and a very pleasant climate here: hills covered with tea bushes and majestic tropical forests characterise the varied landscape on the western side of the *Knuckles Range*. It is also where you will find one of the loveliest hotels in the entire region, the scenically located *Hunas Falls*

By Amaya (31 rooms | tel. 081 4 94 03 20 | www.hunasfallskandy.com | Moderate–Expensive). It is about an hour's drive from either Kandy or Matale to get to the hotel, which is located at an altitude of around 900m (3000ft) and also serves delicious meals.

INSIDER TIP KITULGALA (RIVER KWAI) (137 D1) (*🕮 E13–14*)

The 1956 classic film 'The Bridge on the River Kwai' was not shot in Thailand but here on the *Kelani Ganga*. Alec Guinness won one of the seven Oscars garnered by the exciting drama which is about the construction of a bridge in the Far East during the Second World War. The local children are only too happy to show you exactly where 'Lieutenant Nicholson' got wet. The film bridge is no longer there but the wild river is an ideal place for rafters in their inflatable boats. *On the A7, approx. 1 hour drive to the south*

MATALE (133 E4) (*🕮 F11*)

The bustling district capital Matale (pop. 50,000) is around 25km (16mi) north of Kandy on the A 9 towards Dambulla. The main attraction is the Hindu temple *Sri Muthumariamman Thevasthanam (daily 6am–12.15pm and 4.30pm–8.15pm | entrance fee 200 SLRs)* on Main Street. It was donated by Tamil plantation workers from South India in 1852 and is dedicated to the goddess Mariamman. Its enormous entrance pavilion is completely covered with decorative Hindu images. The ● figures on the façade are every bit as interesting.

Only 3km (1mi) further on the A 9 you reach ★ *Aluvihara*, where it is believed that in the 1st century BC, 500 monks wrote the teaching of Buddha on the leaves of the talipot palm *(ola)* for the first time. The rock monastery comprises several grottos with beautiful murals and terrifying depictions of the Buddhist hell. There is a lovely panoramic view of the mountains from a ☀ *dagoba (daily 8am–6pm | entrance fee 250 SLRs)* slightly higher up.

PERADENIYA BOTANICAL GARDENS ● (133 E5) (*🕮 F12*)

Peradeniya, a suburb of Kandy, is the home of the largest university in the country. The Botanical Gardens, which the British laid out on the site of a former royal pleasure garden in 1824, delights its visitors with the wealth of plant life: avenues of palm trees, bamboo forests, picnic areas. *Daily 7.30am–5pm | entrance fee 1100 SLRs | A 5 towards Gampola, 5km (3mi) from the centre of Kandy*

PINNAWALA (133 D5) (*🕮 E12*)

Orphaned young elephants are reared in this sanctuary and the youngsters enjoying a bath in the Oya River *(10am–noon and 2pm–4pm)* followed by them being fed with a baby bottle make for an excellent photo opportunity. The orphanage is hugely popular and the entrance fee is rather steep. If you want to see something more authentic, you will be much better off seeing the elephants in one of the national parks. *Daily 8.30am–6pm | entrance fee 2000 SLRs | from the A 1 towards Ambukkane, 5km/3mi towards Pinnawala*

NUWARA ELIYA

(137 F1) (*🕮 G14*) **When it the weather is particularly humid and stifling in Colombo (and other places on the plain) in July and August, the middle and upper classes like to seek relief here higher up.**

It is cool here most of the year – and sometimes downright cold. Nuwara Eliya (pop. 43,000) – the name means 'City of Light' – is located at an altitude of 1900m (6234ft) and this means that visitors can enjoy a roaring fire in the hearth in the afternoon and even hot-water bottles in some hotel beds. The golf course on the outskirts of town is considered by some to be *the* Asian golf course. Take a stroll through the pleasant town, discover the English manor house style post office and the Hatton Bank which would not be at all out of place in Kent.

FOOD & DRINK WHERE TO STAY

GLENDOWER

An economical alternative to the busy Grand Hotel and only a few steps away from it: clean, somewhat old-fashioned rooms, pleasant owners, small garden and good – mainly Chinese – cooking. *20 rooms | 5 Grand Hotel Road | tel. 052 2 22 25 01 | Budget–Moderate*

HERITANCE TEA FACTORY ☺

This is a successful example of how an old factory can be converted into a very comfortable hotel. The guests now check in where the tea leaves used to be dried. The spa section includes a sauna; something

visitors really appreciate here at an altitude of 2200m (7218ft). Great importance is placed on environmental protection and social commitment and this is demonstrated through recycling and support for poor Tamils. Those who want to, can slip into a sari or sarong and pluck tea. *54 rooms | in the Kandapola suburb | tel. 052 5 55 50 00 | www.heritancehotels.com | Expensive*

HILL CLUB ★

Here, the elegant lifestyle of yesteryear is still observed: in the evening, the dress code for men is jacket and tie (there are a few loan items available) and drinks are served in the bar amidst the faded splendour of old trophies. *39 rooms | 29 Grand Hotel Road | tel. 052 22 26 53 | Expensive*

JETWING ST ANDREW'S

The hotel is located above the golf course a few minutes' walk from the centre of town. The rooms in the new annex are larger and more comfortable than those in the old colonial building. If it is too chilly outside, you can play a game of billiards in front of the crackling fire in the ● *Road Hole Bar*. The table is more than 120 years old! Hikes with an experienced nature guide are also highly recom-

A VISIT TO A TEA FACTORY

The leaves are fist spread out, known as 'withering' and dried in the factory by means of giant ventilators that blow warm air on them for 10 to 14 hours. The leaves are then rolled, twisted and parted by machines before being laid out on the ground to ferment. After that, the tea is dried, cleaned in large sieves and finally sorted according to the size of the leaves and packed in the characteristic boxes made of light wood. You will be able to try the various types in the factories that cater to tourists and buy your favourite on the spot at very reasonable prices: for example, around 250 SLRs for 200 grams of Broken Orange Pekoe (BOP).

mended. *52 rooms | 10 St Andrew's Drive |
tel. 052 2 22 24 45 | www.jetwinghotels.
com | Moderate*

SHOPPING

You might not think so at first, but the
Bale Bazaar on Main Street is a good place
to do some stress-free shopping. There
are good quality, reasonably priced items

WHERE TO GO

ADAM'S PEAK ★ ● ☼
(137 D2) (*Ⓜ E14*)

This is not the highest mountain on the
island but it is by far the most sacred:
every evening during the season – from
December to March – hundred of pilgrims
tackle the more than 4500 steps to be on
the summit in time to see the sun rise. At

Popular pilgrimage destination: the temple on Adam's Peak

such as warm jackets and trekking pants
available. There is also a wide selection
of saris and other interesting textiles in
shops such as the *Lucky Plaza Emporium*
on New Bazaar Street.

FRANCISCAN PRODUCTS ☺
The nuns of the Franciscan Convent sell
homemade marmalade, chutney and fruit
wine in their small shop. Your purchase
will help them to fund their many chari-
table activities, including schooling. *11 Long
Street, behind St Xavier's Church*

the top, at a height of 2243m (7359ft),
there is a large footprint shaped impression in the rock that is a venerated by
Buddhists, Hindus and Muslims and
Christians alike who all regard the impression to be the foot print of the Enlightened,
Shiva and Adam respectively. The mountain is called *Sri Pada* 'Holy Footprint' in
Singhalese. Depending on your fitness
level, the ascent takes from three to four
hours (starting in Dalhousie). There are
several tea booths along the path where
you can take a brief pause. The closest

Baker's Waterfall on Horton Plains: the plateau has been a national park since 1988

train station is in Hatton and, from there visitors take a bus to Dalhousie (also a train station on the line from Badulla or Kandy). Important: don't forget to take a torch and pullover with you (it is often freezing at the peak before 6am). Start your descent as soon as the sun has risen or you will find it too hot! The INSIDER TIP *Green House (7 rooms | tel. 051 2 22 39 56 | Budget)* in *Dalhousie* just before the first steps is a very simple, but pleasant, guesthouse from where you can start and end the climb. Once you come down, you will be pleased to have a fragrant herbal bath and hearty breakfast waiting for you. You can book both in advance.

HAKGALA ☆
(137 F1) (*山 G14*)

This botanical garden with lotus ponds and avenues of acacia trees is only 5km (3mi) southeast of Nuwara Eliya on the A 5. The altitude (1700m/5577ft) makes it possible for many tree ferns to flourish here. *Daily 8am–6pm | entrance fee 1100 SLRs*

HORTON PLAINS ★ ● ☆
(137 F2) (*山 F–G15*)

Today, lovers of nature hike through rhododendron and fern forests where the British colonials once used to hunt leopards. Although the high plateau is not even 30km (19mi) from Nurawa Eliya, getting there can take quite some time – by car via Belihul Oya (lovely rest house) or by train from Nanu Oya (Nuwara Eliya's station, 10km/6mi from the centre) to Ohiya. The highlights are *Baker's Waterfall*, ☆ *World's End* and ☆ *Lesser World's End* (1000m/3280ft and 60m/1968ft respectively). You should try to be there as early as possible in the morning because fog usually sets in later. *Daily 6am–6pm | entrance fee US$25*

INSIDER TIP SECONDARY ROUTE
TO KANDY ☆ (133 F5–6) (*山 G13–14*)

This highly varied route through the highlands starts north of Nuwara Eliya and runs through such tiny villages as Rikillagaskada, Hanguranketa and Marassana. Rice fields, breathtakingly beautiful terraces and jungle-like thickets line the route. There are also spectacular views of the gigantic reservoirs in Randenigala and Victoria.

RATNAPURA

(137 D2) *(⌖ E15)* **Ratnapura translates as the 'City of Gems' (pop. 60,000) and is 100km (62mi) from Colombo.**
The city has much more to offer than just a look at the glittering treasures from below the surface of the earth – among others, a beautiful location on the southern foothills of the highland area close to Adam's Peak. The Buddha of Viniharama watches over the city from a hill and the god Saman protects the faithful in the *Maha Saman Devale*, 4km (2.5mi) to the west on the A 8. Sections of the pretty temple building date back to the 17th century. There are also many gemstone mines scattered throughout the region around Ratnapura.

SIGHTSEEING

GEM BANK & GEMMOLOGICAL MUSEUM ●
Here you will not only be able to admire particularly beautiful sapphires, tourmalines, rubies, emeralds and amethysts but also be able to see how the gems are excavated and processed. The complex includes a restaurant. *Daily 8.30am–5.30pm | free admission | 6 Ehelopala Mawatha*

WHERE TO STAY

KALAWATHIE
A simple hotel in a very pleasant location. In addition to its large garden, it offers massages, meditation and herbal baths, and also organises hiking tours. *18 rooms | Polhengoda | tel. 045 2 22 24 65 | Moderate*

RATNALOKA TOUR INNS
This hotel is beautifully located 6km (4mi) out of town in a rubber plantation; it has a pool and its own so-called gem museum. *53 rooms | Kosgala/Kahangama | tel. 045 2 22 24 55 | Budget–Moderate*

WHERE TO GO

SINHARAJA FOREST RESERVE
(137 D–E4) *(⌖ E–F16)*
This last 44mi² large area of rainforest on the island is included on the list of Sri Lankan nature reserves as a strictly protected biosphere conservation area. 95 per cent of all of Sri Lanka's endemic birds live here as well as more than half of all Ceylonese mammals. However, leeches are also frequently part of how visitors experience nature here – in spite of that the guestbook is full of rapturous comments. You have to take part in a guided hike on one of the three *Nature Trails* (between 4 and 14km/ 2 to 9mi). If you arrive from Ratnapura, the entrance is near *Kudawa;* the Mediripitiya entrance is most convenient for visitors from the south coast. *Entrance fee 675 SLRs, nature guide from 600 SLRs | information: Forest Department in Colombo (tel. 011 2 86 66 26)*
A rather whacky hotel the **INSIDER TIP** *Boulder Garden (Sinharaja Rd, Kalawana | tel. 045 2 25 58 12 | www.bouldergarden. com | Expensive)*, a 20-minute jeep ride from the Kudawa entrance, is aimed at well-heeled jungle tourists. The eight rooms and two suites are – as the name says – nestled in boulders and natural caves. Motto: eco-luxury in a cave. The spring water pool is part of the Grotto Restaurant. You can stay considerably cheaper and more traditionally in the family-run *Martin's Lodge (9 rooms | 4km from Kudawa gate | tel. 045 5 68 18 64, tel. 042 2 22 55 28 (c/o Post Office) | Budget).*

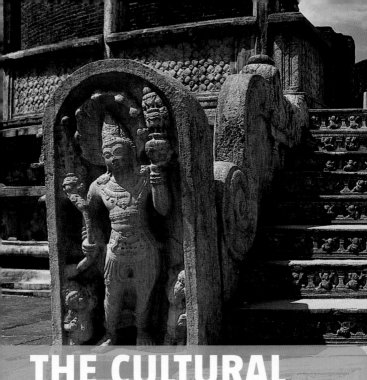

THE CULTURAL TRIANGLE

Here, in the northern centre of the country, there is very little to remind you of the lush tropical coastal landscape and the verdant green mountains of the highlands. And yet this hot, dry region is the home of the most important testimonies of the golden age of Sri Lankan culture and civilisation.

Even though the shape is not absolutely correct, this region is known as the Cultural Triangle today. As Rajarata 'Country of the Kings', its importance radiated far into the Asian continent for over 1500 years and attracted Buddhist pilgrims from Burma and China, as well as merchants from India and Persia.

This is where you see gigantic stupas and impressive statues of Buddha in extensive monastery complexes, beautiful rock paintings like those of the 'cloud maidens' in Sigiriya, or stories of Buddha in the spectacular cave temples of Dambulla, enchanted hermitages such as Aukana and Ritigala and the two cradles of Buddhism on the island in Mihintale and the sacred bodhi tree in Anuradhapura. The kings and artists, architects and workers drew their spiritual strength and inspiration from this religion.

A sophisticated irrigation system (that still astounds experts today) was what made life possible in this part of the is-

Photo: The temple complex in Polonnaruwa

A sacred tree, 'cloud maidens' and the ancient royal reservoirs – the Cultural Triangle does full justice to its name

land interior. Some of the ancient artificial lakes – which the British called tanks and the Singhalese *wewas* – have been reactivated in recent years. They give the landscape its scenic appeal, which is otherwise characterised by boulders that jut up out of the flat green ground. From time to time, it is even possible to see wild elephants crossing the less-frequented roads.

The main attractions and important sights in the Cultural Triangle are spread out and far from each other and it is therefore a good idea to hire a car and an experienced driver. If you do not want to change your hotel frequently and would prefer to have a home base for your excursions, you should look for suitable accommodation in Habarana and between Sigiriya and Dambulla.

ANURADHA-PURA

▓▓ MAP INSIDE BACK COVER
(129 D–E4) (*m E7–8*) **This oldest and most important royal city was the capital of a Singhalese kingdom for well over 1000 years from the 3rd century BC to AD 1017.**
All of the places of interest in the extensive ruins – covering more than 15mi² –

temples, the rice growers in the area did not forget the most important sacred object in this centre of Buddhism. They continued to care for the offshoot of the tree under which it is believed that Buddha found enlightenment. The English 'discovered' the old royal city in 1820 and started excavations there 100 years ago. Today, the holy precinct of Anuradhapura once again attracts Buddhist pilgrims and cultural tourists from all over the world. The modern city next to the park-like field of ruins has a population of around 70,000.

Pilgrims at the Tree of Enlightenment, the sacred bodhi tree, in Anuradhapura

date from this period. They are almost all relics of sacred buildings because, during that time, only temples, monasteries, *dagobas*, halls and courts were built out of stone. Nothing remains of the mud huts and wooden palaces from antiquity, but the walls and outlines give one a good impression of the once thriving metropolis. After Tamil invaders destroyed the city in 1017 it sank into decline. Although the jungle overgrew the ruins of most of the

SIGHTSEEING

The main *dagobas* and the three large, scenic reservoirs in the old part of the city are quite far apart so a bicycle is the ideal means to tour the ruins and most of the accommodations have them for hire *(from 250 SLRs a day). Entire complex open daily from sunrise to around 7.30pm | entrance fee US$25 | tickets available at the Jetavana Museum*

ABHAYAGIRI

The gigantic the 1st century BC temple complex was the nucleus of Mahayana Buddhism, a reform movement. A large *dagoba* stands in the centre but is almost completely overgrown. The complex includes the statue of a meditating Buddha *(Samadhi Buddha)*, a purification bath *(kuttam pokuna*, double bath), the remains of a monks' assembly house (jewel palace from the 8th century) and a statue house *(Mahasena Palace)*, with the island's INSIDER TIP ▶ most impressive moonstone, a semi-circular stone with animal and plant ornaments, in front of the steps leading into it. In order to get an overview of what was once a 495 acre monastery complex, it is a good idea to first of all visit the *Abhayagiri Museum* that has a model of the monastery, as well as Buddha figures and inscriptions, on display. *Daily 10am–5pm | entrance included in ticket price*

ARCHAEOLOGICAL MUSEUM

Finds from the sacred district are displayed on the two floors of the museum and in the open air. *Thuparama Mawatha | Wed–Mon 8am–5pm, closed on public holidays*

BODHI TREE
(SRI MAHA BODHI) ★

Gautama Siddharta became Buddha, the Enlightened, while sitting under this kind of fig tree *(ficus religiosa)* in Bodhgaya in northern India. Since then the tree has been regarded as sacred and it has been called the bodhi tree (tree of knowledge or enlightenment) throughout Southeast Asia. Sri Maha Bodhi in Anuradhapura, an offshoot of the historic bodhi tree from northern India, is believed to be the oldest tree in Asia. It stands on a pedestal surrounded by a golden fence. Pilgrims visit it all day long but especially during the prayer ceremonies that are all announced with a drum roll: around 6am and 10.30am

and then again in the twilight after 6pm. *Daily | entrance fee 200 SLRs*

ISURUMUNIYA

The rock temple is located near the royal pleasure garden close to Lake Tissawewa and the rest house. It dates back to the 3rd century BC. The most important sights are the reliefs in the rock showing bathing elephants and 'The Lovers' a sculptural masterpiece from the 5th or 6th century. It is on display in the small museum next to the temple *(daily except holidays, 8am–5pm | entrance fee 200 SLRs)*.

JETAVANA VIHARA & MUSEUM

This was once the highest *dagoba* in the country and measured 115m (377ft). It

---

★ **Bodhi Tree (Sri Maha Bodhi)**
An offshoot of Buddha's tree of enlightenment that is probably the oldest – certainly the most sacred – tree in Asia → p. 77

★ **Dambulla**
Cave temple complex with statues and wall paintings created over the centuries → p. 81

★ **Minneriya National Park**
This nature reserve is famous for its large elephant population → p. 82

★ **Gal Vihara**
These Buddha statues never fail to fascinate visitors → p. 83

★ **Sigiriya**
Impressive culture and nature – the steep climb is one of the great experiences of any trip to Sri Lanka → p. 86

MARCO POLO HIGHLIGHTS

was overgrown for a long time and after extensive renovation work is now – a still impressive – 71m (233ft) high. The domed building from the 3rd century was the centre of one of the three major monasteries and the home of a strict reformist

RUWANWELI SEYA

This impressive white *dagoba*, which is also known as the *Maha Thupa* (Great Stupa), was built during the reign of the national hero King Dutthagamani in the 2nd century BC, but only completed after his death.

The 3rd century Thuparama Dagoba is the oldest on the island

order under King Mahasena. The reliefs on the altarpieces at the axes of the *dagoba* are very beautiful. The *Jetavana Museum* is only a stone's throw away and, with its valuable finds from the monastery grounds, including pieces of jewellery and golden ornaments, well worth a visit. *Daily 8am–5.30pm | entrance included in ticket price*

MIRISAVATIYA

After he came to power, King Dutthagamani (161–137 BC) had this *dagoba* erected – supposedly above his sceptre – sometime around 150 BC. *Not far from the Tissawewa rest house*

Restoration work began around 100 years ago but was only finished about 40 years ago. A rock crystal glitters on its golden spire. The faithful lay offerings of flowers in front of the four altarpieces that the hanuman langur monkeys then pounce on with glee. The outer wall of the platform is decorated with 350 stone elephants.

THUPARAMA

The oldest *dagoba* on the island was commissioned by King Devanampiya Tissa who was the first to convert to Buddhism. Today's appearance of the dome, under which a splinter of Buddha's collarbone is preserved, dates from 1862.

MUSEUM OF POPULAR ART

Musical instruments and costumes, as well as handicrafts and farming and kitchen equipment, are displayed in this museum. *Sat–Mon, Wed and Thu 9am–5pm, closed on holidays | entrance fee included in ticket price*

INSIDER TIP ▶ WEWAS

This is the name given to the artificial lakes that have provided irrigation for the dry areas in the centre of the island since ancient times. Three large *wewas*, including the oldest in Sri Lanka, *Bassawakkulama*, that was built almost 2500 years ago, glisten in the ruins in Anuradhapura. The other two are *Tissa Wewa* (a popular lake for bathing) and *Nuwara Wewa* (a paradise for water birds).

CITADEL

The open complex borders on the Thuparama Dagoba to the north. The still visible walls once surrounded the king's palace, the Temple of the Tooth and an alms house – the only remnant of this is an 8m long stone trough which was used to distribute rice to the needy and the monks.

FOOD & DRINK

The large hotels serve the best food. Your rice and curry on the 🌿 veranda of the *Grand Tourist Holiday Resort (4 b/2 Lake Road | tel. 025 2 23 51 73 | Budget)* is accompanied by a lovely view of the lake.

WHERE TO STAY

GALWAY MIRIDIYA

Cheerful hotel with a lovely garden and renovated rooms with views of the Nuwara Reservoir – the most beautiful of the modern hotels. *38 rooms | Rowing Club Road | tel. 025 7 21 36 26 | www.galway.lk | Budget*

LITTLE PARADISE

Pleasant guesthouse with individually decorated rooms with balconies; tucked away on a side street behind a large square. Good curries cooked by the owner's family. *6 rooms | 622/18 Godage Mawatha | tel. 025 2 23 51 32 | www.little paradiseanuradhapura.com | Budget*

PALM GARDEN VILLAGE

Very agreeable house around 4km (2.5mi) from the ancient royal city with 40 rooms and 10 suites in a spacious complex with a large pool. *Puttalam Road, Pandulagama district | tel. 025 2 22 39 61 | www.palm gardenvillage.com | Budget–Moderate*

HOTEL RANDIYA

This very appealing hotel is well run and centrally located. *14 rooms | 394/19 A Muditha Mawatha | www.hotelrandiya.com | Budget*

INSIDER TIP ▶ TISSAWEWA RESTHOUSE

25 large, but very simple and – unfortunately – rather overpriced rooms with ceiling fans and mosquito nets over the beds. The romantic, almost 100-year-old, house has an inviting veranda on the ground and first floors, a dining room (where good curries are served) and a park where monkeys and birds make quite a racket. The hotel is in the sacred district and that means absolutely no alcohol! Reasonable prices for hiring bicycles, around 250 SLRs a day. If you stay here, you will be able to admire the *dagobas* in the moonlight. *30 rooms | Old Town | tel. 025 2 22 22 99 | Budget*

WHERE TO GO

AUKANA (129 E6) (𝄞 E9)

Near Kekirawa, halfway between Anuradhapura and the caves in Dambulla, the road turns off the A 9 to the west and

Sila Rock in Mihintale: the birthplace of Buddhism on Sri Lanka

then travels past the *Kala Wewa Reservoir*, which has provided about 100 villages with water for more than 1500 years. The reservoir has a magical atmosphere, especially in the early morning and in the late afternoon. If you have time, you should go for a stroll along the shore road. The real goal of this detour is the ● *Aukana Buddha* (50km/93mi from Anuradhapura). The figure was hewn out of the rock it leans on sometime between the 5th and 8th century – the experts are still quarrelling about the exact date. Its height of 12m (39ft) makes it the largest freestanding statue from ancient times in Sri Lanka (with the base, it measures approximately 14m/46ft) and – along with the statues of Gal Vihara in Polonnaruwa – it is the most impressive. The dedicated abbot of the monastery is building a school for the rural population and welcomes any donations. *Daily 7am–6pm / entrance fee 750 SLRs*

MIHINTALE ☀ (129 E4) (*∅ E7*)

A *dagoba* at the peak of this holy mountain commemorates the meeting between King Devanampiya Tissa and the Indian monk Mahinda. This relative and emissary of the great Emperor Ashoka of India converted the King of Anuradhapura to Buddhism. That was sometime around 250 BC shortly after Devanampiya Tissa's inauguration. Since that time, the expansive complex of painted caves, temples, *dagobas* and ancient cisterns has drawn the faithful to this place 12km (7mi) to the east of Anuradhapura.

A broad exterior staircase leads into the sacred precinct. Before it, a path branches off to *Kantaka Cetiya,* the remains of the oldest *dagoba* in Mihintale. It was probably built in the reign of King Devanampiya Tissa, the first Sri Lankan Buddhist. It continue upwards to the steep Sila Rock. The best time to visit this fascinating site is shortly before 8am when it is not too hot and also not too overcrowded. *Daily / entrance fee 500 SLRs*

YAPAHUWA (133 C–D2) (*∅ D10*)

The impressive rock fortress nestles against a mountain slope 75km (46mi) south of Anuradhapura not far from the major junction in Maho. In the 13th century, it was frequently used by threatened rulers as a place of refuge. Yapahuwa then lost its importance and became a home for hermit monks. There is still a monastery at the site today. Although the fortifications and palace complex have almost completely disappeared, the steep open staircase is in a fairly good state following extensive restoration work. The stonemasons used the South Indian style when they added very beautiful decorations to the steps. The two guardian lions, which are also depicted on the Sri Lankan ten rupee banknotes, are the symbol of the fortress. *Daily 8am–6pm | entrance fee 500 SLRs*

DAMBULLA

(133 E2) *(∅ F10)* ★ � **Monks still live in this temple. The path over the bare rocks to the famous caves can be very strenuous when it is hot, but it is well worth the effort!**

The wonderful panoramic view from the entrance to the caves (at around 340m/1115ft) more than makes up for all your exertion – and the paintings and statues inside more than compensate for the difficult ascent. Five caves, which monks have painted and decorated with statues of Buddha over a period of 2000 years, are open to the public. The oldest works of art originate from the pre-Christian era, the most recent from the 20th century. However, in some of the caves – especially the first, the 'Cave of the Divine King' *Devaraja* – the paintings have suffered from the centuries of smoke from candles and incense. The most impressive sight in the first grotto is a 14m (46ft) reclining Buddha statue – as large as the dying Buddha of Gal Vihara in Polonnaruwa. The second and largest grotto is domi-

nated by a standing Buddha in a pose similar to that in Aukana. One more feature: the mountain water drips incessantly – the mysterious spring does not stop, even in the dry months.

If you go without a guide then remember to take a torch with you (tour guides always carry them). The heat makes the ascent very strenuous at midday. *Daily from sunrise to sunset | entrance fee 1500 SLRs*

The best place to stay is in one of the hotels around the nearby Kandalama Wewa, especially the ☺ INSIDERTIP ► *Heritance Kandalama (162 rooms | tel. 066 5 55 50 00 | www.heritancehotels.com | Expensive)*, that stretches for about 1km up against the mountain and offers a great deal of luxury with its pools, restaurants and spa. It was designed by Sri Lanka's most famous architect Geoffrey Bawa and has received many awards for its high ecological standards (own water treatment plant, sophisticated recycling system). Another good address is the 130,000ft² large *Amaya Lake (tel. 066 4 46 15 00 | www.amayalake.com | Expensive)* complex with 92 Chalets and several eco-lodges, a swimming pool and Ayurveda treatments.

WHERE TO GO

NALANDA GEDIGE ● (133 E3) *(∅ F11)*
It is well worth making a detour from the A 9 (towards Matale and Kandy) to visit this South Indian style statue house with a special history. It is about 24km (15mi) to the south of Dambulla, exactly in the geographical centre of the island. The building has stood on the banks of the Mahawel for at least 1000 years. Nalanda Gedige was under flood threat when plans were made to dam the longest river in the country. The action taken – modelled on that in Abu Simbel in Egypt –

saved the temple: it was removed stone by stone, stored for a few years, and then in 1980 it was rebuilt on an island in the new reservoir.

The statue house displays both Hindu and Buddhist elements and there are even – rather unusual in Sri Lanka – erotic reliefs similar to those India experts know from Khajuraho and Konarak. These and other depictions, especially on the outside walls, make it clear to historians of art and religion just how important Mahayana Buddhism once was on the island. *Free admission*

HABARANA

(133 F1) (*ØØ G9*) **The small village in the heart of the Cultural Triangle lies at the junction of the A 6 (Kurunegala–Trincomalee) and A 11 national roads between Anuradhapura and Polonnaruwa.** Habarana is an ideal place to spend the night before setting out to explore all of the sights in the Cultural Triangle. It is only 52km (32mi) to Anuradhapura, 30km (19mi) to Dambulla while Polonnaruwa is 49km (30mi) away and Sigiriya 22km (13mi).

Apart from a reservoir, Habarana itself has no special sights but the *Minneriya National Park* (9km/6mi) with its many elephants and the hermitage in *Ritigala* (18km/11mi) are not far away.

FOOD & DRINK WHERE TO STAY

CHAAYA VILLAGE HABARANA
Spacious complex surrounded by greenery. Many leisure-time activities, including birdwatching at the nearby Habarana Wewa, are on offer. *106 rooms | tel. 066 2 27 00 47 | www.cinnamonhotels.com/ ChaayaVillagehabarana.htm | Moderate*

CINNAMON LODGE HABARANA
Lovely chalet-style hotel in a park-like garden with swimming pool and tennis courts. Good restaurant. *141 rooms | at the reservoir | tel. 066 2 27 00 11 | www. cinnamonhotels.com/CinnamonLodge Habarana.htm | Moderate*

WHERE TO GO

MINNERIYA NATIONAL PARK ★
(133 F1–2) (*ØØ G9*)
The 21965 acre protected area around the *Minneriya Wewa* is home to numerous water birds, sambar deer and wild elephants. Sometimes more than 100 pachyderms congregate around the edge of the reservoir for an **INSIDER TIP** *elephant gathering* in the dry season between June and October. The entrance to the national park is 9km (6mi) east of Habarana on the road Polonnaruwa. The *Kaudulla National Park* stretches out further to the north. *Entrance fee US$15 plus additional costs and taxes*

RITIGALA ●
(133 E1) (*ØØ F8–9*)
Jungle feeling, ancient ruins, the remote location – the Ritigala environmental protection area is an enchanted site in the middle of the Cultural Triangle. The mountain, with a height of 766m (2513ft), towers over the wide plain and, as a *Strict Nature Reserve,* only its base is accessible. That is the site of the remains of more than 1000-year-old hermitages where the *Pamsukulika*, a group of forest monks, once lived their ascetic lives in complete seclusion. An approximately 600m (2000ft) long path takes visitors past the remnants of a pond, a ritual bathing tank and a platform for walking meditation. The ruins can be reached via a small road off the A 11 to Anuradhapura. *Free admission*

POLONNA-RUWA

(134 B2) *(⬚ H9)* **The origins of this second royal city, and World Heritage Site, lie in the distant pre-Christian times.**

This place actually served, under different names, as the residence of the rulers of Anuradhapura for brief periods in the 4th, 8th and 10th centuries. But what is today described as the Polonnaruwa era only began with the destruction of Anuradhapura. In the 11th century, King Vijaya Bahu first of all drove the Cholas, a Tamil dynasty, out of Polonnaruwa. The magnificent buildings, canals and parks his successor, Parakrama Bahu (1153–86), had constructed founded the fame of this second metropolis.

However, Polonnaruwa's heyday did not last very long: the Tamils once again invaded in 1211 and the city was abandoned in 1314, its fate given over to the jungle, and it fell into oblivion. As was the case with Anuradhapura, it was the English once again who began excavations in the 19th century. Modern Polonnaruwa is a nondescript small district capital with around 15,000 inhabitants.

SIGHTSEEING

The ruins cover an extensive area but the paths to the ancient sights are well signposted; they make pleasant walking and there are several shady resting places. If you have the time, then the best way to explore the large grounds **INSIDERTIP** on a bicycle. Many of the hotels at the reservoir have bicycles for hire at a reasonable price *(300 SLRs per day)*. If you only have one day in Polonnaruwa, you should concentrate on the following main highlights *(daily 7am–6pm | entrance to the historical*

The reclining, 12m (39ft) long, statue of the dying Buddha in Polonnaruwa

sites US$25, tickets can be bought in the museum)

GAL VIHARA ★

The main attraction in Polonnaruwa comprises of four Buddha statues, in complete harmony with the surroundings, carved into a long granite rock. Protected by a rather unattractive roof, they bear witness to the high level of sculptural art in 12th century Sri Lanka. Masterly: the two perfectly proportioned Buddhas in a meditative pose. Enigmatic: the standing

although only parts of the old wall of this round temple remain standing, it is still very impressive. Here, the four statues of Buddha looking at the four entrances play a decisive role. The *Thuparama,* the best

Buddha statue in Giritale, only a few miles from Polonnaruwa

figure with the hand in an unknown position (possibly added later). Release: the 12 m (39ft) reclining Buddha on a beautiful round cushion, with a lotus pattern, indicates that he has attained Parinirvana.

HOLY QUADRANGLE

The ruins of several temples lie in the centre of the former sacred precinct. The oldest, *Atadage,* was built around the year 1100 as the Temple of the Tooth. Somewhat later, this relic, which is venerated in Kandy today, was moved to the much larger, also rectangular, *Hatadage.* Visitors are always astounded at the remnants of the *Vatadage* to the south of this:

preserved and probably oldest building in all of Polonnaruwa, is also worth closer inspection. The roof of this erstwhile 'House of Buddha Pictures' reminds one of temple buildings in South India. The *Gal Pota,* the 'Stone Book', stands in one corner of the quadrangle next to the Hatadage, here King Nissanka Malla had his heroic deeds engraved on the massive block of stone (8m/26ft long, almost 1.4m/4.5ft wide).

KING'S STATUE

The statue of the king is about ten minutes' walk away from the ruins. The ☀ path along the crest of the reservoir has lovely views of rice fields, the rest house and the ruins. The relief-like figure carved out of the rock shows a bare-chested, bearded man with a satisfied expression. Both hands hold a long object pointing towards the viewer – a palm-leaf manuscript, a yoke? That is not clear just as it is not certain – as often claimed – that this statue really depicts the great King Parakrama Bahu.

LANKATILAKA

This ancient image and statue house is majestic with impressive dimensions, approximately 50m (164ft) long and almost 20m (66ft) wide. The columns that frame the path leading to a – now headless – standing Buddha soar about 16m (52ft) upwards. *Kiri Vihara,* the 'Milk Dagoba', rises up to the north of these ruins whose name means 'Lanka's Jewel'. The dome received its name and its gleam by being plastered with shell limestone to give it its white sheen – a symbol for the purity of Buddhist teaching.

MUSEUM ●

This museum is well worth visiting not only because it provides a good overview of the importance and development of the former royal city but also because its air-conditioning provides relief from the midday heat. Models reconstruct the way the various monuments used to look and the exhibits bear witness to the high artistic level achieved in those days. There is also a fascinating collection of bronze Hindu statues including extremely beautiful examples of Shiva dancing. *Daily 9am–6pm | ticket included in entrance fee*

PALACE DISTRICT

The remains of the palaces of Kings Parakrama Bahu I and Nissanka Malla can be seen to the northwest of the rest house: halls, baths and fortress (citadel).

FOOD & DRINK WHERE TO STAY

REST HOUSE

Romantic location on the reservoir. The ten rooms are large and simply furnished, the atmosphere on the veranda is very pleasant and the food is good (including fish from the lake). *tel. 027 2 22 22 99 | Budget*

HOTEL SUDU ARALIYA

Accommodation particularly suitable for families, with a spacious garden directly on the reservoir; 30 pleasant rooms, large pool. *New Town | tel. 027 2 22 48 49 | www.hotelsuduaraliya.com | Budget–Moderate*

WHERE TO GO

GIRITALE

(134 A2) (*𝄞 H9*)

The nature reserve and bird sanctuary on two ancient reservoirs is 11km (7mi) prior to Polonnaruwa. This is an ideal starting

LOW BUDGET

▶ The *Lake Wave Hotel (522/31 Lake Road, Stage 2 | tel. 025 3 77 25 25 | www.lakewavehotel.com)* on Kumbichchan Kulama near the new bus terminus in the south of Anuradhapura, only has four rooms but is a good choice for travellers on a budget.

▶ You can stay comfortably and cheaply at the *Devi Tourist Home (5 rooms | Lake View Watte, New Town Road | tel. 027 2 22 31 81)* in Polonnaruwa.

Fables painted on rock: the graceful 'cloud maidens' of Sigiriya

point for nature and wildlife viewing – also possible on a bicycle. Several comfortable hotels in the vicinity make for a relaxing break between sightseeing; the loveliest is the *Deer Park (tel. 027 2 24 62 72 | www.deerparksrilanka.com | Moderate)* with a fabulous pool complex.

INSIDER TIP MEDIRIGIRIYA
(134 A–B1) (*ftJ H8*)
This round temple (40km/25mi north Polonnaruwa), which was donated by King Aggabodhi IV (reigned 667–683) from Anuradhapura, is not often visited by tourists. There was probably a monastery at the site as early as in the 2nd century. Each of the four statues of Buddha in the middle of the sanctuary is surrounded by eight columns in alignment with the points of the compass. There are additional ruins in the hilly surroundings. The scenic drive to Medirigiriya passes along an ancient canal and the main rice growing region in the Cultural Triangle. The ancient irrigation system makes it possible to harvest the valuable grain twice a year in this area.

SIGIRIYA

(133 F2) (*ftJ G9*) ★ ☼ **Visible from afar, this ochre coloured flat-topped rock formation rises straight up from the surrounding plain.**

Its name is synonymous with a world-famous symbol of Ceylonese high culture: the *Cloud Maidens of Sigiriya* from the 5th century AD, colourful frescos whose charming beauty definitely compensates for having to climb a steep path half way up the mountain. The most pleasant time to set out is 8 o'clock in the morning because the tourist groups do not usually arrive until after 9 o'clock. Some stone steps and a narrow spiral staircase lead up to a viewing platform and the gallery on the rock face with the famous 'cloud maidens'. The young women, with naked upper bodies and flowers and fruit in their hands, have charmed visitors for centuries. Are they princesses, servants or nymphs? They could also be – as many art historians believe – *apsaras* or celestial beings.

THE CULTURAL TRIANGLE

Those who find the climb to the plateau at the peak too strenuous can admire the view from the middle platform. You can buy refreshments and postcards there where the steep path to the summit begins between two stone lion's paws. There is an impressive ☼ view over the jungle from a height of 200m (656ft). It is worthwhile visiting the museum near the main entrance where models and exhibits will give you an idea of Sigiriya's importance during the course of history. *Daily 7am–5pm | individual ticket US$30*

FOOD & DRINK WHERE TO STAY

REST HOUSE
In the typical style of simple colonial inns. A good place for a curry or tea break after visiting the rock. *13 rooms | in the centre of Sigiriya | tel. 066 2 28 62 99 | Budget*

HOTEL SIGIRIYA ☼
Pleasantly located establishment with a view of the rock and with a swimming pool. *80 rooms | tel. 066 2 28 68 21 | www.serendibleisure.com/hotelsigiriya | Budget*

SIGIRIYA VILLAGE ☼
More comfortable than the Sigiriya; terraced bungalows with a spacious garden and pool. The Ayurvedic centre offers excellent massages. *124 rooms | tel. 066 2 28 68 03 | www.forthotels.lk | Moderate*

JETWING VIL UYANA
The spacious ecological resort is located 10km (6mi) to the west of Sigiriya. The 24 bungalows stand on stilts surrounded by a wetland of lakes and reed beds. Good spa, interesting excursion programme and plenty of wildlife around the resort. *Tel. 066 4 92 35 84 | www.jetwinghotels.com | Expensive*

BOOKS & FILMS

▶ **Anil's Ghost** – This novel (2001) by Michael Ondaatje, who was born in Sri Lanka, bursts with imagery and also displays sensitivity for the beauty and tragedy of the island

▶ **Running in the Family** – The bestselling author describes the history of the extended Ondaatje family in a – sometimes – humorous way. The memoir is set in the pre-war Ceylon (published 1997)

▶ **Heaven's Edge** – The novel (2005) by Romesh Gunesekera depicts Marc's breathtaking odyssey through the homeland of his childhood

▶ **A Year in Green Tea and Tuk-Tuks** – A charming and interesting account of journalist Rory Spowers' (2007) time in Sri Lanka setting up an organic farm

▶ **Death on a Full Moon Day** – The award-winning film from 1997 – original title, *Puruhanda Kaluwara* – by Prasama Vithanage tells the story of a father who does not want to believe that his son has died (available from *www.vithanage.com*)

▶ **The Bridge on the River Kwai** – David Lean's World War Two classic was shot on the Kelani Ganga near Kitulganga in 1956

THE EAST COAST

Sri Lanka's eastern landscape is one of rocks, savannah, jungle, artificial lakes and lagoons. Some of the country's most beautiful beaches stretch out along the coast: Nilaveli near Trincomalee, Passekudah and Kalkudah, 30km (19mi) north of Batticaloa, as well as the surfing hotspot of Arugam Bay south of Pottuvil. Here, INSIDER TIP the bathing season runs from May to September, the time when the monsoon rains are pouring down on the west coast. The years of civil war have left their traces and there are still army checkpoints here and there but, as a whole, a relaxed atmosphere can now be felt in the region. Improvements in the infra-structure and an increasing number of good accommodation options now make it an easy matter to travel in the east. Certainly the friendly locals are very happy to see the return of tourists.

ARUGAM BAY/ POTTUVIL

(139 F2) (*M14*) This area suffered greatly from the civil war and the 2004 tsunami but ★ Arugam Bay has once again attracted the enthusiastic surfer community from around the world.

Photo: Hindu temple in Trincomalee

New beginnings in the east – after the end of the civil war, Sri Lanka's east is back on the tourist map

The gently curved bay is considered one of the very best surfing areas. Travellers can choose between simple budget accommodation and pleasant bungalow complexes.

MUDU MAHA VIHARE

You can cycle to the 'Great Monastery by the Sea' the *Mudu Maha Vihare*, set in the dunes at the southern edge of the nearby Muslim village of Pottuvil. Ruins, columns and a *dagoba* rise impressively out of the sand. The main attractions are a 3m (10ft) large Buddha and two Bodhisattva statues turned towards him in the former statue house. This indicates the influence of Mahayana Buddhism on the monastery that was probably built in the 5th century. *Daily | free admission*

Plenty of sun and excellent swell make Arugam Bay a top destination for surfers

FOOD & DRINK
WHERE TO STAY

INSIDER TIP HIDEAWAY

Friendly resort; not directly on the beach but on the other side of the road around three minutes from the sea. Good food and the friendly staff guarantees a pleasant atmosphere. *5 rooms and 7 cabanas | tel. 063 2 24 82 59 | www.hideawayarugam bay.com | Budget*

SIAM VIEW

A cheerful multicultural group runs this resort at Surfer's Point. The Siam View has only three simple rooms. The restaurant serves good Thai cuisine and there are cool drinks and delicious draught beer at the beach bar where parties are frequently held. *Mobile tel. 0773 20 02 01 | www.arugam.com | Budget*

STARDUST

For more than 20 years, the Stardust was *the* hotel on Sri Lanka's southern east coast and the proprietor, Per Goodman, enjoyed legendary status. The tsunami destroyed almost everything and Per and two members of the staff lost their lives. But his wife Merte keeps up the good work and the restaurant now once again offers the Danish and tropical specialities it was renowned for. *8 rooms in the main house, 3 cabanas | www.arugambay.com | Budget–Moderate*

LEISURE & BEACHES

330 days of sunshine a year, water temperatures between 24–28 °C (75–82°F) and waves up to 4m (13ft) high are the reasons for Arugam Bay's reputation as a top surf destination. The surfers make their way past the huts with the – mainly Muslim – fishermen repairing their nets to one of the ten surf spots along the mile-long bay. The narrow beach is not always clean and the strong breakers mean that it is only suitable for experi-

enced swimmers. If you do not have your own board with you, it is usually possible to hire one from your hosts. The *Arugam Bay Surf Club (c/o Fawas Lafeer | tel. 077 9 55 22 68)* is one of companies that offer courses.

WHERE TO GO

INSIDER TIP ▶ KUMANA NATIONAL PARK
(139 E–F 3–4) (*ω L–M 15–16*)

The 69mi² large Kuman National Park is a mere 40 minutes' drive south of Arugam Bay. It forms the northern border of the huge Yala Nature Reserve. The reserve has five sections and its many lagoons and the Kumana Reservoir make the national park an important refuge for birds. The 255 bird species include grey pelicans and giant storks. Elephants and golden jackals also make their paths through the dry landscape of the savannah. The drive takes you via Panama to Okanda, where there is both the entrance to the park as well as also the Hindu *Okanda Malai Murugan Kovil* an important rest station for pilgrims on their way to Kataragama. *Daily 6am–6pm | entrance fee 2500 SLRs*

LAHUGALA-KITULANA NATIONAL PARK ● (139 F2) (*ω M14*)

The smallest national park in Sri Lanka covers an area of 5.5mi² and stretches for around 18km (11mi) along the A 4 west of Puttuvil. The protected area was only established in 1980 and serves as a corridor between the Yala East and Gal Oya National Parks. The chances of coming across a herd of elephants there are particularly good between August and October – and, with some luck, you can even see them from the A 4. However, bird lovers will also be delighted at the more than 100 species. The visit can be combined with Magul Mahu. *Daily | free admission*

MAGUL MAHU (139 E2) (*ω L14*)

Head along the A 4 to the west, and after about 8km (5mi) there is a signposted left turn off that heads into a savannah and jungle landscape. It is not uncommon for elephants to cross the road here. The ruins of a Buddhist monastery rise up in the middle of the jungle. It was built by King Dhatusena of Anuradhapura in the 6th century and renovated in the 14th. There are a couple of friendly caretakers who look after this gigantic complex and they will be happy to show you around. *Daily | free admission*

INSIDER TIP ▶ PANAMA
(139 F3) (*ω M15*)

The village, a good 12km (7mi) south of Arugam Bay, is the final stop on the surfaced road towards the Yala National Park; however, it is only passable during the dry months. 'Paanama' – that is how it is pronounced – is a Singhalese village that has managed to retain its authentic character. The people living there are friendly but reserved. You should plan to

---

⭐ **Arugam Bay**
A real highlight for surfers – the secluded bay has one of the world's best breaks → p. 88

⭐ **Fort Frederick**
One of the most important Hindu shrines on the island, the Thiru Koneswaram Kovil, lies within the walls of the Dutch fortress → p. 93

⭐ **Nilaveli**
Sri Lanka's leading hotel groups have big plans for the picture-perfect stretch beach north of Trincomalee → p. 94

MARCO POLO HIGHLIGHTS

make this excursion in the afternoon when your chances of seeing enormous crocodiles sunning themselves on the sandbanks in the small watercourses are better. An unbelievably colourful bird world lives around a lake 3km (2mi) to the west of the village.

BATTICALOA

(135 E3) (🛱 L10) Tourists rarely make their way to the second largest town on the east coast, even though the road connection is now rather good. So far, there are only modest accommodation options in Batticaloa.

In spite of this, the boat people in the lagoon hope that guests will soon start coming again to travel out with them at night to listen to the 'singing fish'. The locals explain that the way to do this is to put your ear on the rudder when this is held in the still water. After many attempts, the author has still not been able to experience this miracle. While the majority of the fishermen in this area are Tamil Christians, the rice growers – also Tamils – are members of the Hindu religion. Muslims also live in the small town; most of them as merchants and truck drivers.

The town's main attraction is the formidable *Dutch Fort* that dates back to 1682, whose entrance gate is adorned with two rusty cannon barrels and the coat of arms of the Vereenigde Oostindische Compagnie (VOC). Several authorities have their offices in the interior. The INSIDER TIP beautiful beaches in the surroundings, such as nearby *Kallady Beach,* are almost deserted but Sri Lanka's most famous shipwreck 17km (11mi) off the coast is a great attraction for divers. The 'HMS Hermes', the world's first aircraft carrier, has rested 60m (197ft) below the surface of the water since being destroyed in an attack by Japanese military aircraft in 1942.

WHERE TO GO

PASSEKUDAH AND KALKUDAH
(135 E2) (🛱 L9)
The beaches at Passekudah and Kalkudah, around 30km (19mi) north of Batticalao, were among the most popular seaside resorts on the east coast until the beginning of the 1980s. However, they were abandoned for decades as a result of the civil war. Now the government has developed an ambitious plan of action to reawaken the sleeping beauties. Work on new resorts is being carried out with great diligence and some have already been opened, including the chic and expensive *Maalu Maalu Resort & Spa (40 rooms | Passekudah | tel. 065 738 83 88 | www.*

LOW BUDGET

▶ A second-class train ticket from Colombo to Trincomalee costs even less than 900 SLRs. You can make a break in Habarana or at Gal Oya Junction to visit the main sights in the Cultural Triangle.

▶ The Shahira Hotel on Nilaveli Beach, only a few hundred feet from the sea, offers simple but pleasant rooms with verandas and ceiling fans at very reasonable prices. Friendly service. *28 rooms | tel. 026 5 67 02 76*

▶ The pleasant and affordable Arugambay Surf Resort is right on the beach and is geared towards surfers. *12 rooms | tel. 063 2 24 81 89 | www.arugambay.lk*

Meeting place – the market is a good place for a game of cards

maalumaalu.com | Expensive) with modern bungalows, minimalistic design and a large swimming pool.

TRINCOMALEE

(131 E5) *(ɱ J6)* **This would actually only be a dusty, nondescript coastal town (pop. 22,000) if not for Swami Rock and the Hindu sanctuary of Koneswaram.**

The vibrant town is on a bay with a beautiful natural harbour surrounded by hills (and guarded by the navy). It has a lively ferry port, rural suburbs and some beautiful beaches that stretch from the town to the north. *Trinco,* as the locals call it, was frequently bitterly fought over in the 1980s and 1990s. Either the 'Tigers' sank government ships or the government sank theirs. Today, the situation is calm and the well developed A 6 makes it possible to reach the heart of the Cultural Triangle within a two-hour drive along the east coast from Habarana. The interesting landscape also makes the **INSIDER TIP** train trip a fascinating experience.

SIGHTSEEING

FORT FREDERICK ★

All of the important sights are located on a peninsula between Dutch and Back Bays and can be easily explored on foot. The cape that juts out into the sea here is almost completely covered by Fort Frederick that has borne the name of the then Duke of York since 1803. The *Thiru Koneswaram* towers up 130m (427ft) above the sea at the tip of the promontory. This Hindu temple is dedicated to Shiva and was only reconstructed in 1952; the Portuguese had destroyed it centuries before and started using its stones to build the fort in 1624. The fortress was later used by the British and, today, functions as a barracks for the Sri Lankan Armed Forces. The *Thiru Koneswaram Temple* from the golden age of Tamil rule on the east coast is said to have 1000 columns. Remnants of what was once the most magnificent Hindu temple on the island can still be seen in the surf at the foot of the rock. The greatly revered *lingam*, a fertility symbol and one of Shiva's forms, in the present temple originates from the earlier building and was rescued from the sea by divers. Spectacular ceremonies are held every day at 7am, 11.30am and 4pm. If you want to take photographs, ask for permission beforehand.

Visitors are usually terrified when they look down into the raging depths from the highest point of the fort, *Swami Rock*. This lookout point is also known as ☀ *Lover's Leap* because Francina Van Rheede hurled herself into the sea from this spot in 1687; jealousy, unrequited love... The story has a happy end; the young Dutch woman survived the fall. *Daily | free admission | entrance through a gate on Fort Frederick Road*

PATHIRAKALI AMMAN KOVIL

Another Hindu temple consecrated to Kali, the patron goddess of Trincomalee, is not far from the entrance to the fort, on Dockyard Road opposite the Esplanade with the McHeyzer Stadium. The *Pathirakali Amman Kovil* dates from the 11th century and – together with the smaller *Kali Kovil*, also dedicated to the vengeful deity in front of it – impresses with its colourful and richly decorated portal tower. Based on South Indian models, these entrances, which are also known as *Gopuram*, are intended to recall all of the many stories of Indian mythology. *During the day | free admission*

FOOD & DRINK
WHERE TO STAY

There are a few modest eateries in the city including the garden restaurant *Trinco Village (246 Dockyard, corner of Dyke Street | Budget)*. If you feel like tasty Italian food for a change, the *Palm Beach Resort (12 Alles Garden | Budget)* on Uppuveli Beach is a good option but don't forget to reserve in advance!

CHAAYA BLUE TRINCOMALEE

The resort from the 1970s has been radically renovated and was relaunched in 2010. With its 81 rooms and chalets and a large swimming pool, it offers perfect relaxation on lovely Uppuveli Beach. Tip: the boat excursions to Muttur or dolphin watching. *81 rooms | tel. 026 2 22 23 07 | www.cinnamonhotels.com/ChaayaBlu Trincomalee.htm | Moderate–Expensive*

WELCOMBE ☀

The top hotel in town was built by a British planter in 1936 and has a spectacular view of the natural harbour. The food is excellent, with a great selection of delicious seafood. *26 rooms | 66 Orr's Hill | tel. 026 2 22 23 73 | www.welcombehotel.com | Moderate*

WHERE TO GO

KANNIYAI (131 E4) (*m J6*)

About 4km (2.5mi) to the west on the A 4, towards Anuradhapura, seven ● hot springs bubble up from of the otherwise bone-dry soil. The springs have been a pilgrimage site for centuries as it is believed that the waters have miraculous powers. Asia's oldest epic the 'Ramayana' mentions the springs as the place where the evil giant Ravana met with his end. He had kidnapped Sita, the beautiful wife of the Indian Prince Rama, and taken her to Sri Lanka. Rama was only able to rescue her with the help of an army of monkeys. In his anger, Ravana rammed his lance into the ground and wept seven hot tears – and they then turned into the seven hot springs. *Daily | free admission*

NILAVELI ★ (131 E4) (*m J6*)

The most famous beach on the east coast starts 15km (9mi) north of Trincomalee. There has been a real sense of optimism here since the end of the civil war an increasing number of accommodation options. Popular destination for an excursion: *Pigeon Island (3500 SLRS per boat, entrance fee 2000 SLRs),* 300m from the beach. The trip is organised by the hotels and freelance boatmen. It is also possible to go whale watching. The *Scuba Diving Centre (www.scubasrilanka.com)* arranges diving trips to the Coral Garden or Red Rock to the north. Families will feel at home at the *Nilaveli Beach Hotel (80 rooms | tel.*

off (at 45km/28mi) left to the village of Tiriyai a further 3km (2mi) away. You reach the entrance to the temple after a drive of 1.5 km (1mi) along a sandy track. It is believed that the temple columns that frame a small reliquary shrine (*dagoba*) date from the 8th century. Eight hairs of Buddha, which the Enlightened gave to two merchants as a gift, have been revered there from time immemorial. *Daily | free admission*

Traditional lifestyle in a dream location: Tamil fishing village at Nilaveli

026 2 23 22 95 | www.tangerinehotels.com | Moderate) with a swimming pool and pleasant open-air restaurant making it one of the most popular hotels. The *Pigeon Island Beach Hotel (tel. 026 4 92 06 33 | www.pigeonislandresort.com | Moderate),* with swimming pool and 44 stylish rooms and suites, is also recommended.

INSIDER TIP ★ **TIRIYAI** (131 D3) (*ℳ H5*)
The ruins of a temple on a hill near the hamlet of Tiriyai, around 35km (22mi) north of Nilaveli, are the destination of this interesting day trip. From the picturesque coast road north a path branches

UPPUVELI (131 E4) (*ℳ J6*)
The 5km (3mi) long beach in Uppuveli begins north of Trincomalee and attracts many budget tourists, despite the fact that there is a limited number of inexpensive establishments. One of the recommended venues is the *Sea Lotus Park Hotel (54 rooms | tel. 026 2 22 53 27 | www.lotustrinco.com | Budget–Moderate).* The *Commonwealth Soldiers Cemetery* in the nearby village of Sampalthivu commemorates the victims of the Japanese attacks in 1942 when Trincomalee was the most important marine base of the British colonial forces in the Indian Ocean.

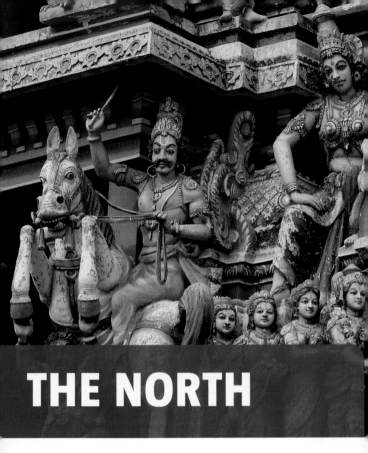

THE NORTH

The Jaffna Peninsula, which juts out into the sea like a cat's claw, surprises visitors with a vibrant Tamil culture and interesting landscapes. Traces of the decades-long civil war are still visible but the locals are facing the future with great optimism.

There is little in the way of tourist infrastructure but those who make the long journey – there are 400 strenuous kilometres (250mi) between Colombo and Jaffna – will be richly rewarded. In addition to the colourful Hindu temple, Nallur Kandaswamy Kovil, there are also many colonial buildings to admire in the Tamil metropolis, while the barren islands in the Palk Strait have an atmosphere all their own. There is a fascinating dune landscape near Sri Lanka's northernmost Point Pedro and you will meet friendly, interested people wherever your travels take you.

JAFFNA

(126 C2) (𝓝 C1) At first sight, the metropolis (pop. 160,000) in the north does not appear very inviting: dusty streets and war-damaged buildings everywhere. The strong military presence also does not help put visitors in a cheerful holiday mood. In spite of that, a visit is worthwhile. The shops are full of beautiful,

Photo: Perumal Kovil in Jaffna

The heartland of Tamil culture – the north was closed to tourists for decades but now the region attracts the more adventurous

colourful saris and the television channels broadcast Indian soap operas. The temple bells ring at Hindu prayer times and Buddhist Sri Lanka seems a very long way away indeed.

SIGHTSEEING

Several churches, including the *Rosarian Convent* on Convent Road and the mas-sive *St Mary's Cathedral* on Main Street, recall the old colonial past. In the past, business life flourished around the elegant clock tower that can be seen from far away – until the building was destroyed in the war, as was the famous *Jaffna Public Library*. It was set ablaze by a Singhalese police unit in 1981 and 97,000 documents were lost forever. The building, which was modelled on an

Revered by Hindus: the
Nallur Kandaswamy Kovil

Indian mogul palace, was not reopened
until 2004 *(can only be viewed from outside)*.

FORT

The star-shaped fortress on the edge of the
Jaffna Lagoon is developing into something of a tourist attraction. But a great
deal still needs to be done; many buildings
in the interior of the complex were destroyed in battles between the Sri Lankan
Army and LTTE at the beginning of the
1990s. Built by the Portuguese in 1618, the
fort owes its present appearance to the
Dutch who captured Jaffna in 1658. A
British garrison was housed here between
1795 and 1948 and the fort continued to
be used for military purposes after independence. In addition to the renovation
of the bastions, the former commander's
residence *Queen's House* and *Kruys Kerk*,
built in the form of a cross and consecrated
in 1706, are currently being restored. *Access
via a gate on Beach Road*

NALLUR KANDASWAMY KOVIL ★

It would be worth visiting Jaffna just to see
the Hindu sanctuary in the northeast of
the town. It is dedicated to the god of war
Murugan (Skanda) and is one of the five
most important places of Hindu pilgrimage in Sri Lanka. From afar, the elegantly
curved roof of the *Nallur Kandaswamy Kovil*
is an impressive sight. The origins of the
temple are unclear. As in other places, the
Portuguese also destroyed this religious
site in 1620. While the oldest sections of
the complex (as we see it today) date back
to the middle of the 18th century, the
striking red and white striped wall was not
erected until the year 1909. The interior is
divided into two, a covered courtyard with
water basin on the south side and the
main sanctuary with various individual
shrines on the north. Especially during the
Nallur Festival, which begins on the sixth
day after the full moon in July and lasts
four weeks, tens of thousands of pilgrims
make the journey to Jaffna. Then, the
temple complex is flooded with a sea of
people visiting the daily processions. Men
are only allowed to enter the interior bare-
chested and photography is not allowed.
The atmosphere during the solemn ceremonies at 5am, 10am, noon, 4pm and 5.45pm
is very special. *Daily 5am–noon and 4pm–
8pm | free admission | Temple Road*

FOOD & DRINK
WHERE TO STAY

There are few decent restaurants; the best
are those in the hotels. The *Cosy Restaurant
(Budget)* on a side street off of Stanley
Road serves hearty Indian food and tasty
Jaffna curries.

BLUE HAVEN

The air-conditioned rooms are a bit drab,
but clean, and the service is friendly. Two
pluses are the pool and the quiet location.

9 rooms | 70 Racca Road | tel. 021 2 22 99 58 | www.bluehavenjaffna.com | Budget

JAFFNA CITY HOTEL
At the moment, this hotel is the best place to stay in Jaffna. A modern building, with fairly plush rooms, sauna, gym and good restaurant. *10 rooms | 70/6 K.K.S. Road | tel. 021 2 22 59 69 | www.cityhoteljaffna.com | Moderate*

WHERE TO GO

THE ISLANDS
(126 A–B 2–3) (*ΩΩ A–B 1–2*)
A trip to the islands, in the shallow waters of the Palk Strait, is a must. Sparsely populated and – as a result of the low rainfall – with little vegetation, they have a unique atmosphere. Three of them – *Karaitivu, Kayts* and *Punkudutivu* – are connected by a causeway. The largest island, *Kayts,* is in the sea opposite Jaffna. *St James Church,* erected in 1716, in the main town of the same name, is worth closer inspection. *Chaddy Beach,* in the south near the village of Velanai, is not ideal for bathing. The ferries to *Nainativu* and *Delft* depart from the island of *Punkudutivu* that is also connected by a causeway. Known by the Singhalese as *Nagadipa* (Snake Island), Nainativu is one of the most important Buddhist places of pilgrimage in the north of the country; according to the legend, the Enlightened personally came to the island to settle a conflict between the Snake King and his nephew. Today, a permanently decorated stupa commemorates this visit. The ferry takes about one hour to reach Delft Island. However, apart from the Delft ponies, there is not very much to see on the 19mi² large island. *Karaitivu,* which the Dutch used to call 'Amsterdam', is definitely much more interesting on account of its secluded ★ *Casuarina Beach.* The narrow, sandy

beach – lined with the Casuarina trees that gave it its name – stretches along the island's north side as far as the lighthouse. So far, no accommodation is available.

KANTARODAI (126 C1–2) (*ΩΩ C1*)
About 12km (7mi) north of Jaffna in the village of Kantarodai, not far from Chunnakam, is the unique *Purana Maha Raja Vihara* sanctuary with 20 hemispherical miniature stupas. It is possible that a Buddhist monastery was located here between the 2nd century BC and 13th century. The stupas are up to 2m (6.5ft) high and once housed the mortal remains of the monks.

POINT PEDRO ★ (127 D1) (*ΩΩ D1*)
There are no sights in Sri Lanka's most northerly town itself but the interesting landscape en route makes the trip worthwhile. The Hindu temple *Sri Selvachchannithi Kovil* near the airport makes an interesting stop. The Manalkadu sand dunes stretch towards the east and the nearby fishing villages, which were damaged in the tsunami, have since been reconstructed.

★ Nallur Kandaswamy Kovil
Admire the colourful world of the gods in Jaffna's most important Hindu temple → p. 98

★ Casuarina Beach
Although it might not be as beautiful as the beaches on the east coast, Casuarina Beach will still tempt you to take a dip in the sea → p. 99

★ Point Pedro
The landscape en route to Sri Lanka's northernmost spot is very impressive → p. 99

MARCO POLO HIGHLIGHTS

TRIPS & TOURS

The tours are marked in green in the road atlas, the pull-out map and on the back cover

FASCINATING TEMPLE TOUR AROUND KANDY

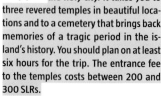

Culture, history and romance characterise this excursion into the area surrounding the holy city. It takes you to three revered temples in beautiful locations and to a cemetery that brings back memories of a tragic period in the island's history. You should plan on at least six hours for the trip. The entrance fee to the temples costs between 200 and 300 SLRs.

You can take this approximately 50km (31mi) long tour in your own car or in one of the omnipresent three-wheelers (about 4000 or 2000 SLRs respectively). The starting point is the little-visited **Kandy War Cemetery**, on the Deveni Rajasinghe Mawathe in the Dodanwala district. You can reach it by car if you take the route to the university suburb of Oeradeniya and then turn towards Aniwatta/Katugastota at Maheweli. This is where 201 soldiers of various British Empire troops are laid to rest – most of them fell between 1942 and 1945 in their attempts to ward off the Japanese invasion. The rows of graves are separated by religion. The Commonwealth War Graves Commission ensures that the lawn is always trimmed and the surround-

---

Photo: Tea plantation in the mountains

A temple tour around Kandy and a train trip through the mountain region – culture and nature are waiting for you in Sri Lanka

ing greenery creates a wonderful tropical feeling, as well as one of contemplation over the transience of the world.

The first of the three temples of this tour is **Embekke Devale**. The road to this sanctuary branches off from the – always busy – Colombo-Kandy road to the west of Peradeniya in Polgahamula and continues for around 7km (4mi) on a good, winding road past rice fields, towering coconut palms and simple farmhouses to the south. The sacred site is dedicated to the god of war, Skanda (Kataragama to the Singhalese) who, according to Hindu mythology, is one of Shiva's sons and the brother of the elephant-headed deity Ganesha. As the guardian god of the island, there are shrines, known as *devales*, dedicated to him in many places including Embekke. The 32 intricately carved columns with their attractive depictions in the so-called Hall of Drummers are especially noteworthy. Valuable Ceylonese ironwood is just one of the materials that was used to make them. The hall, which is open at the sides, probably dates from the 17th century and may have been an audience hall for the regents who had their residence in nearby Gampola at the time. However, Hindu-Buddhist melange: while the eastern section is devoted to the Enlightened and has highly detailed murals dating from the 17th century on the ceiling and walls, almost half a dozen Hindu deities are venerated in the western part. The u-shaped corridor contains five niches with altars in honour of Vishnu (in the middle), Saman (on the left side), Kataragama on

The hilltop temple at Gadaladeniya has splendid views

King Vikramabahu III, who ruled the small kingdom in the mountains between 1357 and 1374, is believed to have been the original benefactor. You will be able to admire the great skill of the woodcarvers in the nearby village of Embekke where there are many small workshops.

The **Temple of Lankatilaka** dominates the landscape from its position on a rock 2km (1mi) northwest of Embekke. As the inscription of King Bhuvanekabahu IV shows, its origins date back to the year 1344. The main building is an interesting a peacock (rear left), Vibhishana, a brother of the Ravana, the king of the demons (right side) and one where the elephant god Ganesha is worshipped (rear right). If the massive brick building happens to be closed, ask for the person with the key. He is almost always somewhere on the grounds.

Finally, 3km (2mi) to the north and also on a rise, there is the **Temple of Gadaladeniya** with a magnificent view of the hills nearby. The building, which was also erected in 1344, displays South

Indian style elements possibly – as inscriptions show – because the architect was a Tamil called Ganeshvarachari. The frieze that was chiselled into massive stone blocks along the entrance area is decorated with beautiful elephants and dwarves. There is also a rock trough with water lilies, a bodhi tree, a shrine in honour of Vishnu – usually closed – as well as a stupa with tapered roof in the typical Kandy style in the grounds. After you leave the Gadaladeniya Temple, you can drive 2km (1mi) back to Kandy via Peradeniya on the national road number 1. It is worth making a short stopover in the nearby village of Kiriwalula where the people specialize in brass handicrafts. The famous Botanical Gardens → p. 69 are on the wayside and are worthy of a lengthy visit.

2 SCENIC TRAIN RIDE THROUGH THE MOUNTAINS

★ The train chugs leisurely through tea and banana plantations, over viaducts and through tunnels, past spectacular gorges and unforgettable views of the wild landscape – the railway line from Colombo to the highlands is one of the most beautiful in Asia. The train trip from the capital city to the final destination of Badulla takes about ten hours.

The Colombo railway station in the early morning is full of crowds jostling everywhere. Thousands of commuters get off the trains and head toward their workplaces while throngs of shoving passengers try to get on the waiting trains. The 'Little Girl', the *Podi Menike*, starts its all-day trip to the mountains shortly before 6am. To the rear of the train is the observation saloon, with large windows to take in the passing scenery. The first top is Gampaha, a small town that does not have much of interest except the pretty botanical gardens

just outside of the city limits, Henaratgoda. The tropical paradise became famous when the first rubber trees, which had been smuggled out of Brazil, were planted here in 1876 and started a boom. Thereafter the landscape becomes more hilly, tropical, and lush: rice fields turn into rice terraces and there are patches of jungle on both sides of the tracks.

The Ihalakotte Pass, approximately half way along the 121km (75mi) stretch from the capital to the former royal city, makes great demands on the two diesel locomotives pulling the express with its aged, rust-brown coloured carriages. But, this makes it possible for the passengers to enjoy the magically beautiful landscape at leisure.

Two or three tunnels and then the 798m (2618ft) high Bible Rock can be seen looming up out of the densely forested hills; a prominent flat topped mountain that looks like a thick open book known as *Batalegala* by the Singhalese. Now, the railway track runs along a precipice for a short while before the train pulls into the Peradeniya Junction station. From here, it is only a few miles to Kandy → p. 63 and only a few hundred yards to the renowned Botanical Gardens → p. 69. But the journey continues via Gampola, Hatton, Nanu Oya (this is the station for Nuwara Eliya but it is actually 10km (6mi) out of town), Bandarawela and Ella to Badulla. Railway fans consider this one of the most beautiful routes in Asia, if not the world. The route has many interesting things along with the fabulous scenery (for example, in Gampola, where a water-level indicator shows how high the floodwaters of the Maheweli River sometimes rise). The view in Hatton is of a seemingly endless bright green carpet of tea, interrupted only by the yellow blossoms of the acacias that have been planted between the tea bushes to provide some shade. If you decide to get off in the lofty city (at an altitude of 1271m/4170ft), you can take the picturesque road via **Dickoya** and the **Castlereagh Reservoir** to **Dalhousie** at the foot of the pilgrimage mountain Adam's Peak.

The train continues on its journey and soon the light changes and becomes darker

important Stonycliff Estate. As is the case with many other plantations, such as Mackwoods and Rothschild, it still bears its old colonial name. But, the money the women receive for their work also comes from a distant age: they are still on the bottom rung of the income ladder.

The train makes a lengthy stop in **Nanu**

Colourful saris in endless fields: a tea picker working on a tea plantation

when the locomotive struggles through the Poolbank Tunnel – with a length of 562m (1844ft), the longest in Sri Lanka. Don't put your camera away yet; soon after you pass ✂ **Kotagala**, only 8km (5mi) north of Hatton, you will have a spectacular view of the St Clair's and Devon Waterfalls that thunder into the depths surrounded by tea plantations. With luck, you might also see the Tamil tea pickers working in the midst of the endless rows of bushes. In this region, many of them belong to the historically

Oya where buses, taxis, three-wheelers and rental cars wait for visitors who have **Nuwara Eliya** → p. 69, the old summer resort frequented by the English, as their final destination. Note the beautiful village sign in the rustic train station with its beautifully curved Sinhalese and Tamil letters. Continuing further eastwards, the landscape changes into one of giant ferns, rhododendron forests and banana plantations. Not far away is the unique landscape of **Horton Plains** → p. 72 that has been a UNESCO World Heritage Site since

2010. The train reaches the highest point of 1897m (2943ft) between **Pattipola** and **Ohiya**. The spectacle of nature outside the carriage windows becomes increasingly more dramatic – deep gorges and then villages where it almost seems as if the train is steaming through the local vegetable market. The bustling trading city **Bandarawela** → p. 62, **Ella** → p. 60, whose fabulous location on a mountain slope attracts so many backpackers, and then the final leg over monumental bridges – one with nine arches is also known as the 'Nine Hearts Bridge' – followed by yet another highlight, an enormous curve, the only switchback loop in the Sri Lankan railway system. The *Demodara Loop* offers the perfect opportunity for photographing the full length of the train from the window of your carriage. It is said that a simple peasant provided the troubled engineers of the Graig & Cockshott Company the bright idea for solving a technical problem. He suggested winding the railway line around the mountain like a turban. The journey ends in the late afternoon when the train arrives at the centre of the tea industry **Badulla** → p. 62 at an altitude of only 680m (2231ft) in the heart of Uva province. The railway station and small town has real colonial charm: wrought-iron garlands and benches, as well as the green guardhouse form an ensemble that seem to have been imported from merry old England. Here, you will be able to relax and think about the history of the construction of this 290km (180mi) main railway line. Only three years after the then Governor Sir Henry Ward solemnly opened the first leg from Colombo to Ambepussa 54km (34mi) away, the first steam locomotive was able to make the journey to Kandy. In 1885 Nanu Oya was added to the network and Bandarawela followed in 1894. However, the first train did not steam into Badulla

until 1924. The First World War and the following financial crisis had repeatedly delayed further construction and building the line was also in no way a simple matter. Ultimately, 46 tunnels had to be cut through the various mountains along the route. As early as in 1875, the engineer M.T. Doyne had to justify the exploding costs: 'The strenuous and expensive work, such as drilling through hard rock and the many boulders at the bottom of the mountains, as well as the high embankments along the valley and ravines simply make this unavoidable'. When the work was completed, however, the owners of the tea plantations had every right to rejoice as they were then able to transport their bales easily and relatively inexpensively in wagons to the harbour in Colombo.

This train journey is just as scenic in the opposite direction. Holidaymakers with only a limited amount of time can opt to do just the most picturesque stretch which runs between Bandarawela and Nanu Oya (approximately three hours travelling time). If you have hired a car and driver, you can send him ahead with your luggage and be collected at your destination – a memorable and inexpensive way to add a new highlight to your trip around the island.

The *Podike Menike* sets out from Colombo Fort every day at 5.55am, the *Udarata Menike* at 9.45am. Departure in Badulla is at 5.45am and 8.50am. Depending on the distance travelled, a first-class ticket in the *Observation Saloon* costs 750 SLRs and should definitely be reserved in advance. Seats 21, 22, 43 and 44 are next to the windows. The price for the comfortable Rajadhani *(www.blueline.lk)* and Expo Rail *(www.exporail.lk)* carriages is up to 2250 SLRs (incl. meals). It is not possible to reserve seats in the not very comfortable – but entertaining – 2nd and 3rd class carriages. But, they are dirt cheap.

SPORTS & ACTIVITIES

Most tourists do not think of the island as a typical destination for sports activities but enthusiasts will be able to be active in a surprising number of ways.

BALLOON FLIGHTS

Take to the skies for a spectacular view over the reservoirs, rice fields and – above all – the mountain fortress in Sigiriya in the Cultural Triangle. A hot air balloon flight is an unforgettable experience and these are some of the organisation that provide them: *Adventure Asia (tel. 011 5 86 84 68 | www.ad-asia.com)*, *Air Magic (tel. 011 7 26 24 42 | www.airmagic.lk)*, *Sun*

Rise in Lanka Ballooning (tel. 011 2 89 84 70 | www.srilankaballooning.com).

BIRDWATCHING

Parakeets in the treetops, peacocks on the roofs and pink flamingos in the lagoons – the 236 native and 203 migratory bird species will soon turn any tourist into an amateur ornithologist. The best period for bird watching is from November to April when the migratory birds are in the country. Most of the 33 endemic species can be found in the lower wetlands in the southern part of the island, especially in the *Sinharaja Forest Reserve*. Birds

Golf and cricket, hot air balloon flights and sailing, trekking and bird watching – active holidaymakers will be spoilt for choice

are drawn to reservoirs and lagoons in particular, so good areas are in the *Uda Walawe*, *Kumana* or *Yala West National Parks* while *Bundula*, on the south coast has a great to its variety of marine birds.

CRICKET

Wherever you are in the country, you will be able to see how much fun the young boys and girls have playing cricket on the village squares. When national matches – or international, Asian and World Championships – are played in the large stadiums in Colombo, Galle and Kandy, a match is a must for the festive atmosphere. Every waiter and reception-ist will be able to give you exact dates of upcoming matches. The *Singhalese Sports Club (tel. 011 2 69 53 62)* at Maitland Place in Colombo can tell you all you need to know about playing a match and the highlights of the cricket season.

DIVING

The underwater landscape around Sri Lanka might not be as fascinating as that of the Maldives atolls but there are still many unusual things to see: fascinating canyons and rocks, a great variety of marine life and some famous shipwrecks. You can dive throughout the year: in the winter, off the southwest coast and in the south, and off the east coast – especially near Trincomalee – in the summer months. For a selection of dive centres and dive spots see *www.divesrilanka.com*.

GOLF

The British not only brought their passion for cricket to the island, but also their love of golf. Although there are only three courses, their location and atmosphere will tempt golfers to spend an afternoon on the fairways. Founded in 1879 the *Royal Colombo Golf Club (223 Model Farm Road | tel. 011 2 69 54 31 | www.rcgcsl.com)* is considered the finest and has a lovely location in the east of the capital city. It would be worth making a trip to the *Victoria Golf & Country Resort (tel. 081 2 37 63 76 | www.golfsrilanka.com)* in Ratewella, around a 30-minute drive from Kandy, just to admire the landscape. Surrounded by mountains, the 18-hole course nestles up against the Victoria Reservoir, which it is named after, and also offers comfortable rooms for overnight stays. The *Nuwara Eliya Golf Club (tel. 052 2 22 28 35)*, which was founded in the city in the heart of the highlands in 1889, has conditions similar to those in the Scotland. Beautifully located between the Jetwing St Andrew's, Hill Club and Grand Hotels, it will be hard to work up a sweat at an altitude of almost 2000m (6600ft).

MOUNTAIN BIKING

The hills around Kandy and the mountains near Nuwara Eliya offer excellent conditions (and climate) for mountain bikers. However, hardly any of the hotels have suitable bikes for hire. If you don't want to take your bike with you on the plane, you should contact one of the specialised providers and join in their programmes. You can then cycle through the countryside in a small group. Reliable organisations include the *Eco Team (www.srilankaecotourism.com)* and INSIDER TIP *Lanka Sportreizen (tel. 011 2 82 45 00 | www.lsr-srilanka.com)*, a Belgian company with its offices in Colombo.

NATURE & ECOTOURISM

An increasing number of operators are now offering unusual programmes in the wilderness. In addition to the small specialist enterprises, the eco-branches of the Jetwing hotel company have a good reputation in this sector with camping trekking in Buttala (between Yala Park and the highlands near Ella) and other activities. Information from *Jetwing Eco (tel. 011 2 38 12 01 | www.jetwingeco.com)* in Colombo. Other well known specialists include *Wild Holidays Travel (www.wildholidaystravel.com)* and *Reddot (www.reddottours.com)*, a British nature tour operator that offers canoeing and whitewater rafting trips. The *Eco Team (www.srilankaecotourism.com)* also offers a wide range of activities for mountain bikers, bird lovers and hiking enthusiasts.

SAILING

The dangerous currents and reefs in many

areas mean that sailing is not very widespread in Sri Lanka. However, in several coastal towns some young people and fishermen occasionally offer it from the beach. Experienced yachtsmen can obtain additional information from the *Colombo*

TREKKING & HIKING

It is considerably easier to organise your own hikes – even demanding ones – in the mountains of Sri Lanka than in most of the classic trekking countries in Asia.

There are some great dive sites in the south and east of the island

Rowing Club (tel. 011 2 43 37 58) or *Otter Aquatic Club (tel. 011 2 69 23 08)* in Colombo.

SURFING

Experienced surfers should take their own boards with them as many surfers feel that the quality of the rental boards leaves a lot to be desired. During the summer, surfers from all around the world meet regularly at *Surfer's Point* on INSIDER TIP *Arugam Bay*, on the southern east coast. Here they enjoy excellent surf, peaceful surroundings and ideal weather conditions from April to November.

The most scenic hiking areas, such as *Horton Plains,* the high plateau south of Nuwara Eliya, or the area around the *Hunas Falls* north of Kandy, as well as the *Knuckles,* a rocky landscape south of Kandy, are all suitable for experienced hikers without the help of any organisers or accompanying guides.

However, if you would prefer to go hiking with an international group, *Adventure Lanka Tours (tel. 011 2 36 18 41 | www. adventurelanka.co.uk)* in Colombo and *Eco Team (www.srilankaecotourism.com)* are two organisations offering interesting tours including hikes to caves and through the rainforest.

TRAVEL WITH KIDS

Sri Lankans of all religions and classes adore their children and – in marked contrast to India – this applies to both boys and girls alike. They are just as warm and caring when they meet their guests' offspring. Travelling with children will usually mean a very warm reception and lots of friendly attention from the locals.

Sri Lanka is not a typical family destination and parents (or the family doctor) should decide on whether young children will be comfortable in the tropical climate. However, older children will have a lot of fun in the exotic environment. They can watch the toddy tappers balancing their way from palm to palm to tap the coconuts on the south coast, the cheeky monkeys in some of the temples (such as in Dambulla) or just take in the exotic life on the streets in the bazaars.

THE WEST COAST

EXCEL WORLD ENTERTAINMENT PARK
(136 A1) (*ऻ B14*)
This park is a mini Ceylonese Disneyland but the locals are very proud of it. All ages can amuse themselves with activities such as a bowling alley and a roller skating rink while the smaller children will have more fun at the go-kart track, the merry-go-rounds and other traditional amusements. *Daily 10am–6pm | free admission and a small fee for each amusement | 338 T. B. Jaya Mawatha (Darley Road) near the Town Hall | Colombo*

THE SOUTH

CANOE TRIP NEAR GALLE
(136 C6) (*ऻ D18*)
If the children don't find the ideal of a stroll through the fort in Galle much fun then take them off to the Gin Ganga River for a paddle inland. There is plenty of wildlife to see in the mangroves – especially in the early morning and late afternoon. *Idle Tours | 3000 SLRs per person | 58 Church Street | tel. 077 7 90 61 56 and 077 8 03 47 03 | www.idletours.com*

TURTLE CONSERVATION
RESEARCH CENTRE ☺
(136 B4) (*ऻ C16*)
Five of the world's seven species of marine turtle lay their eggs in the warm sand

Young holidaymakers will find lots to do in Sri Lanka – turtle watching, elephant rides and a paddle through the mangroves

along the coast. The people living there consider them a delicacy and, for this reason, turtle hatcheries have been established for their protection – commercial reasons – making this kind of animal protection not without controversy. At Sri Lanka's oldest, the *Turtle Conservation Research Centre*, visitors can learn many interesting things about these endangered marine animals. The children will be especially fascinated by the freshly-hatched babies in the water tanks. *Daily 9am–6pm | entrance fee 200 SLRs | 409 A Main Street | Kosgoda*

THE HIGHLANDS

ELEPHANT TRANSIT HOME
(137 F3) (*❼ G16*)
Instead of going to the overpriced Pinnawala Elephant Orphanage, you can visit the young animals in the Elephant Transit

Home near the Uda Walawe National Park. They also care for orphaned elephants before returning them to their natural surroundings when they are around four years old. However, it is only possible to visit the – on an average – 30 to 40 jumbos for around twenty minutes at their feeding times: 9am, noon and 3pm. The animal orphanage is only a few miles away from the national park and it is easy to combine a visit to the two. *Entrance fee 500 SLRs*

MILLENNIUM ELEPHANT FOUNDATION
(133 D5) (*❼ E12*)
The camp a few miles away from the elephant orphanage in Pinnawala offers rides on the grey giants. The museum is also worth a visit. *Daily 8.30am–5pm | entrance fee without elephant ride 1000 SLRs, with ride from 2000 SLRs for 15 minutes | Randeniya, Hiriwadunna, Kegalle | www.millenniumelephantfoundation.com*

FESTIVALS & EVENTS

Even more than is the case in other Asian countries, almost all of the major festivities in Sri Lanka are religious in origin. The only 'worldly' festivals are cricket matches – the national sport. Most of the major matches take place between November and March – right in season. Every full moon day *(poya)* is a holiday, public life takes a break and the sale of alcohol is forbidden everywhere. Some *poya* days are celebrated with multi-day festivities and as many as 1 million people take part in the most popular events (in Kandy).

PUBLIC HOLIDAYS

1 January New Year's Day; **4 February** Independence Day; **13/14 April** Singhalese and Tamil New Year Festival; **1 May** Labour Day; **22 May** Day of the Republic; **25 December** Christmas Day; **31 December** New Year's Eve

FESTIVALS & EVENTS

JANUARY
Full moon: ▶ INSIDER TIP *Duruthu Perahera* in Kelaniya (on the northern outskirts of Colombo) a nocturnal parade with elephants, dancers and religious dignitaries commemorates Buddha's supposed visit to the island of Lanka – a legend that is 2500 years old.

FEBRUARY/MARCH
▶ INSIDER TIP *Thai Pongal:* the Hindu festival on the day of the full moon in honour of the sun god.
▶ *Maha Shivarati:* new moon night at the end of February/beginning of March, Hindus celebrate the symbolic union of Shiva with his wife Parvati. Particularly impressive in the Muthumariman Temple in Matale near Kandy.
Full moon: ▶ INSIDER TIP *Navam Maha Perahera* in Colombo. As many as 50 elaborately adorned elephants and several thousand dancers, monks and jugglers.

MARCH/APRIL
▶ *Good Friday and Easter:* Sri Lanka's Christians hold the most spectacular Good Friday and Easter celebrations in Negombo with colourful parades and passion plays.

Processions with decorated elephants, parades full of colour and lively cricket matches – you will really be impressed

MAY

Full moon: ▶ *Wesak:* Buddha's birth, enlightenment and death are celebrated for two days and nights.

JUNE

Full moon: ▶ ⭐ *Poson* festival commemorates the arrival of Mahinda who brought Buddhism on the island. The most impressive celebrations are in Mihintale.

JULY

Full moon: the ▶ ⭐ *Esala Perahera* in Kandy is one of the world's largest religious festivals. Ten days and nights where illuminated elephants make their way from the Temple of the Tooth *(Dalada Maligawa)* through the city.

▶ *Id-Ul-Fitr (Ramadan Festival):* Muslim festival celebrating the end of the fasting period (at a different time each year) an especially large number participate in the festivities in the oldest mosque in the country, the Kachchimalai Mosque in Beruwala.

▶ ⭐ *Kataragama Festival:* every year, tens of thousands make their way to the small town of Kataragama, north of Hambantota, to pay homage to the Hindu god of war Skanda at the time of the full moon in July.

OCTOBER/NOVEMBER

▶ *Deepavali:* the most popular Hindu festival lasts for several days and is held throughout the country at the time of the new moon at the end of October/beginning of November. Among other things, it commemorates the god Rama's return to his town of birth Ayodhya after his victory of the king of the demons, Ravana. The faithful light oil lamps in the temple: *Deepavali* means row of lights.

LINKS, BLOGS, APPS & MORE

LINKS

▶ www.srilanka.travel/best_of_srilanka Everything you want to know about your destination at a glance: itinerary ideas, info about the island's history, cuisine, wildlife, cultural events and videos

▶ www.seat61.com/SriLanka A multi-award winning personal website with lots of train travel information including rail timetables, photographs and tips about train travel in Sri Lanka

▶ www.srilankaelephant.com A website run by a keen wildlife and elephant enthusiast that extensively details the predicament of these magnificent and endangered animals

▶ www.aboutcolombo.lk There is always something interesting going on in the vibrant metropolis and this website is a great guide to the important events in the city. It also offers downloadable maps and videos

BLOGS & FORUMS

▶ www.thesrilankatravelblog.com Blog run by Red Dot Tours with entries by different authors covering current tourist developments and new discoveries

▶ theculturetrip.com/asia/sri-lanka Collection of current articles all about local Sri Lankan culture, art, books, films, music, galleries and theatre

▶ www.tripwolf.com Travel tips, activities, photos, blogs and evaluations from the travel community. Background reports and the possibility of direct bookings for accommodation

VIDEOS

▶ short.travel/sri1 A short video with a title that says it all: 'How to get the best out of the Cultural Triangle'

▶ short.travel/sri2 Video of traditional dancers performing during the Esala Perahera festival held in July/August

Regardless of whether you are still preparing your trip or already in Sri Lanka: these addresses will provide you with more information, videos and networks to make your holiday even more enjoyable

VIDEOS

in Kandy, during the two weeks before the full moon. Fire twirlers, colourfully decorated elephants, whip performances and lavish cultural dances

▶ short.travel/sri3 Travel documentary about the island that includes interesting history, culture and some great pictures from a whale watching trip

APPS

▶ Lanka Traveller A user-friendly Travel Guide App for iPhones, with useful sightseeing info, current events, pictures and descriptions as well as GPS location maps

▶ Sinhala Dictionary Offline Sachith Dassanayake, owner of the www.sachith.co.uk website, developed this handy app for Android smartphones. As the name suggests, the application does not require an internet connection as it works offline

▶ Sri Lankan Recipes Want to know more about Sri Lankan cuisine? Then this iOS and Android app is perfect for you – lots of sumptuous recipes to try

NETWORK

▶ www.facebook.com/aragum This is the ultimate virtual meeting point for surfers, party enthusiasts and fans of Arugam Bay

▶ www.facebook.com/OldeCeylon A trip down memory lane with pictures of the island when it was still called Ceylon. Old photos, historical maps and mementoes posted by history buffs

▶ pwww.lakdasun.org Sri Lankan outdoor enthusiasts exchange reports, videos, photos and information about their activities. Lots of practical tips about hikes and trekking trips

▶ twitter.com/OfficialSLC Cricket is the national sport in Sri Lanka and with the Sri Lankan Cricket twitter account you can get tweets about matches

▶ www.onlinenewspapers.com/srilanka.htm A site that lists links to all the online national newpapers

The Publisher shall not be held responsible for the contents of the links, blogs, apps, etc. listed here

TRAVEL TIPS

ARRIVAL

SriLankan Airlines (www.srilankan.com) has nonstop flights every week from London. Sri Lanka is also included on the schedules of several Middle Eastern airlines including Emirates (www.emirates.com), Etihad (etihadairways.com) and Qatar Airlines (qatarairways.com), with a stop-over in the Gulf. Katunayake Airport is around 35km (22mi) north of Colombo; buses and taxis usually take at least an hour to get to the centre of town. If you are not being collected you can take a taxi, bookings at the counter in front of the entrance and exit – fixed prices with your ticket. Those travelling from the United States and Canada will need to take a connecting flight from the UK or Europe.

BANK & MONEY

Banks are usually open from 9am to 1pm (Mon–Fri). There are cash dispensers (ATMs) with the Maestro and Cirrus symbols in many places. Many hotels and large restaurants accept credit cards as well as foreign currency (euros and dollars).

BUS & TRAIN

There is a well developed public transpor-tation system that is inexpensive – but not especially comfortable. Maintenance and new equipment do not seem to be high on the list of priorities. You can reach almost all destinations in the country by the state-run – usually rust-brown – CTB and SLTB buses. There are private compa-nies that run air-conditioned coaches on the major routes, such as Colombo–Kandy and Colombo–Jaffna. The railway is also well built and inexpensive. Starting in Colombo, the trains travel to the north via Anuradhapura to Vavuniya, to Trincomalee and Batticaloa on the east coast, to Kandy and the highlands, as well as to Badulla and along the cost to Matara via Galle.

RESPONSIBLE TRAVEL

It doesn't take a lot to be environ-mentally friendly whilst travelling. Don't just think about your carbon footprint whilst flying to and from your holiday destination but also about how you can protect nature and culture abroad. As a tourist it is especially important to respect nature, look out for local products, cycle instead of driving, save water and much more. If you would like to find out more about eco-tourism please visit: www.ecotourism.org

CAR HIRE

Hiring a car with a driver is a stress-free, safer, informative and more economical (you need expensive travel insurance if you drive yourself) way to see the country. A car with driver also includes fuel (up to 100km free mileage) and works out at about $55–70 (£35–45) per day. The driver is given an additional $6 a day (called: batta) with which he also pays for his food and lodging (not the responsibil-ity of the client). There is an exception: if your hotel has no separate rooms for driv-ers, you should pay for his simple accom-modation – that will make the rest of your journey more pleasant.

From arrival to weather

Holiday from start to finish: the most important addresses and information for your trip to Sri Lanka

CONSULATES & EMBASSIES

BRITISH HIGH COMMISSION
389 Bauddhaloka Mawatha | Colombo | tel. +49 11 5 39 06 39 | ukinsrilanka.fco.gov.uk/en

UNITED STATES EMBASSY
210 Galle Road | Colombo | tel. +49 11 2 49 85 00 | srilanka.usembassy.gov/visas.html

CUSTOMS

Tourists are allowed to bring in two bottles of wine and 1.5L of spirits into the country. A maximum of 7kg (3kg tax-free) of tea can be taken out of the Sri Lanka. It is forbidden to import or export antiques, weapons, drugs and any protected animal or marine products (tortoiseshell, ivory etc.).

DOMESTIC FLIGHTS

The air taxis operated by *SriLankan Airlines* offer private charter flights, for more information email *airtaxi@srilankan.aero* or *tel. 019 733 13 66.* Heli Tours (395 Galle Road | Colombo | tel. 011 314 49 44) have regular flights from Colombo's domestic airport Ratmalana to Jaffna and Trincomalee. *Deccan Aviation Lanka (tel. 07 77 70 37 03 | www.simplifly.com)* offer helicopter flights.

ELECTRICITY

230–240 volts; the sockets are usually three-pin but can also be square pin so it is a good idea to carry an adapter with you. If you forget to take one along they are inexpensive and widely available in Sri Lanka

CURRENCY CONVERTER

£	SLRs	SLRs	£
1	218	100	0.45
3	653	150	0.70
5	1,088	250	1.10
7	1,523	300	1.40
10	2,175	500	2.30
15	3.263	750	3.40
20	4.350	1,000	4.50
35	7.613	2,500	11.30
60	13.050	4,000	18.00

$	SLRs	SLRs	$
1	130	100	0.80
3	392	150	1.20
5	655	250	1.90
7	915	300	2.30
10	1,300	500	3,90
15	1,960	750	5.80
20	2,600	1,000	7.70
35	4,550	2,500	19.30
60	7,800	4,000	30.80

For current exchange rates see www.xe.com

EMERGENCY NUMBERS

Tel. 011 243 33 33; fire brigade/ambulance: 110; police: 119. If you have a disagreement about prices etc., contact the tourist police *(tel. 011 242 14 51);* usually just threatening to do so will be enough.

HEALTH

Bottled mineral water is widely available, otherwise you should only drink boiled water, forget about ice cubes in your drinks and always peel any fruit you eat. Be careful of open buffalo yoghurt (curd) and ice cream! It is a good idea to refresh your tetanus, diphtheria and polio prophylaxis before you leave home and also be vaccinated against hepatitis A and typhoid. There is only a slight risk of malaria in Sri Lanka and it also helps to stay well covered in the early evening and at night. Most of the doctors and chemists in the large towns are well trained and speak English. The best private clinic in Colombo is the *Apollo Hospital (578 Elvitigala Mawatha, in the Narahenpita district | tel. 0114 53 00 00)* and another highly-respected doctor is *Dr. A. M. Sebastiampillai (166/12 Kirulapone Avenue | Colombo | tel. 011 2514104 (clinic) and tel. 0777 845674 (mobile; only in cases of an emergency!)*

IMMIGRATION

To enter the country it is necessary to have a passport that is valid for at least six months prior to your scheduled departure date; children under the age of twelve need a children's passport. You can apply in advance for a visa or *Electronic Travel Authorisation (ETA)* under *www.eta.gov.lk*, it costs US$20 and is valid for 30 days. Transit passengers and children under the age of twelve are exempt from this fee. It is also possible to apply on arrival for an ETA but there is a surcharge for this service. If you intend to stay longer, you can apply for a three month visa from a Sri Lankan Embassy or via the *immigration. gov.lk* website.

INTERNET INFORMATION

Two comprehensive and informative sites are *www.lanka.net* and *www.infolanka. com*. The government tourism authority provides excellent tips for holidays on the island as well as information on events under *www.srilanka.travel*. Holidaymakers can book exclusive accommodation and excursions under *www.srilankainstyle. com* and *www.reddottours.com*, and *www. go-lanka.com* also provides a list of carefully selected hotels. *Explore Sri Lanka*, the best print tourist magazine in the country, gives a wealth of excellent travel information at *www.explore.lk*. And finally, you can also find out all you need to know about specific locations under sites such as *www.arugambay.com, www.negombo. org* and *www.hikkaduwanet.com*.

INTERNET CAFÉS & WI-FI

The introduction of smartphones has led to a reduction in the number of internet cafés. Internet access rates vary from about 1 rupee a minute in the major towns to about 6 rupees per minute or more in the more remote areas. The number of Wi-Fi hotspots are increasing and nowadays most hotels, guesthouses and cafés offer the service, often free of charge.

OPENING HOURS

Most shops are open from 8.30am to 7pm, Monday to Friday and many also until 1pm on Saturday. The countless small shops in the bazaars and tourist resorts are usually open from around 7am until about 10pm, often seven days a week.

PHONE & MOBILE PHONE

There are telephone shops and internet cafés that provide international calls at very reasonable rates, just look for the ISD/IDD letters. The country code for Sri Lanka is *0094*; to call home from Sri Lanka dial *00* then your country code (UK *44*; USA and Canada *1*). It is usually no problem to use mobile phones but there are many areas with no reception in the mountains. The best idea is to first check the rates with your mobile provider before you travel, it may be cheaper to purchase a local SIM card on arrival at the airport or in one of the many phone shops (you will need your passport). *Dialog* and *Mobitel* are two recommended providers.

PHOTOGRAPHY

As a rule, the local population has no objections to being photographed but you should make sure to ask for permission if you intend to take close-ups. You should exercise restraint at religious ceremonies and you should never have people pose next to images of Buddha as this is a punishable offence! It is also forbidden to take pictures of military establishments and persons in uniform. Be sure to have enough USB sticks and memory cards with you; if not, they can be purchased in specialised shops. Do not forget your charger and adapter!

POST

There are also post offices in small towns and villages *(Mon–Fri 8.30am–4.30pm, Sat 8.30am–1pm)*. Air mail takes between 7 to 10 days to Europe. Postcards cost 25 SLRs, letters up to 20 grams 75 SLRs and it is best to send your mail from post offices as the letterboxes are not very reliable.

PRICES & CURRENCY

The increase in the cost of living has also led to a hefty rise in prices in Sri Lanka in recent years and this is especially true of entrance fees to national parks and archaeological sites. You can also have a rather unpleasant surprise when you take a look at your bills: as many as three dif-

SINHALESE

English	Sinhalese	
Yes/No	Ow/Na	ඔව්/ නෑ!
Please/Thank you	Karunakarala/Istuti	කරුණාකරර./ ඉස්තුති.
Pardon me/Sorry!	Samaavenna!	සමා වෙන්න!
Good afternoon!	Suba davasak!	සුබ දවසක්!/
Good evening!	Suba sandyaavak!	සුබ සන්ධ්‍යාවක්!
Goodbye!	Naevata hamuvemu!	නැවත හමුවෙමු!
My name is ...	Magay nama ...	මගේ නම...
I'm from ...	Mama ... vella	මගේ රට...
I don't understand	Mata terenne na	මට තේරෙන්නේ නෑ.
How much is it?	Gaana kiyada?	ගාණ කියද?
Excuse me, where can I find ...?	Samaavenna, ... koheda?	සමා වෙන්න, ... කොහේද෴කොහේද?

1	eka	එක	5	paha	පහ	9	namaya	නමය
2	deka	දෙක	6	haya	හය	10	dahaya	දහය
3	tuna	තුන	7	hatha	හත	20	wissa	විස්ස
4	hatara	හතර	8	ata	අට	100	siiya	සීය

ferent taxes and fees are added to the net price. In addition to a 10 per cent service charge *(SC)*, expensive hotels and restaurants in particular add a value added tax *(VAT)* of 12 per cent *(standard rate)* or 20 per cent *(luxury rate)* and sometimes even a national building tax *(NBT)* of 3 per cent. But, all in all, the island is still a relatively inexpensive destination when compared with prices at home.

BUDGETING

Tea	around £0.80/$1.40 *for a cup*
Meal	around £2.50/$4.10 *for a dish of curry*
Beer	around £1.20/$2.10 *for a large bottle*
Bus ticket	around £0.20/$0.40 *in the city*
Shirt	around £4.10/$6.90 *for good quality*
Taxi	around £0.60/$1 *per kilometre*

The Sri Lankan currency is the rupee (SLRs) and there are 100 cents in 1 rupee. Bank notes are available in 10, 20, 50, 100, 200, 500, 1000, 2000 and 5000. US$ and euros are accepted in most large hotels and tourist establishments and there are official tourist prices in US$ for entrance fees to national parks and sights.

PERSONAL SAFETY

Safety in the country greatly improved with the end of the civil war in 2009 and it is now also possible to travel to the east of Sri Lanka without any difficulties. However, land mines will continue to be a problem in the north for many years to come. You should also be prepared for a considerable military presence in that region. Before travelling to remote areas, you should check the recommendations made by your Foreign Office. With those exceptions, Sri Lanka is one of the safer tropical holiday destinations. There are almost no assaults on tourists but occasionally pickpockets are active and there might be some cheating. This is due to some naïve holidaymakers who let touts talk them into just about anything. However, there is a particularly ugly aspect which is that Sri Lanka is a well known destination for child sex tourism. So far, the offenders appear to be unconcerned that their crimes can now also be punished in their home country, regardless of where they were committed. Information under www.ecpat.net

THREE-WHEELERS

Taxis are not especially common in Sri Lanka but the popular motorised three-wheelers (also known as trishaws; only tourists call them tuk-tuks) can be found everywhere. Agree on a price before you start your journey. Ask the hotel porter or trustworthy locals about the approximate price. And, be careful if the driver gives you hot tips about shops and accommodation. They are usually only interested in their – rather hefty – commission.

TIME

Sri Lanka is 5.5 hours ahead of GMT and does not follow daylight saving time.

TIPPING

It is customary to give a tip. Porters get from 50 to 100 SLRs, taxi drivers a maximum of 50 SLRs It is appropriate to give up to 10 per cent of the bill if you are satisfied with the service in a restaurant.

WHEN TO GO

The weather is fine from December to March with the best period from mid-January to the end of February. April and May are hot and humid. The rainy season on the west coast is from mid-May to August and sometimes into October. It is dry on the east coast from around May to September. Temperatures on the coasts reach 30°C (86°F). It is somewhat cooler in Kandy and the humidity is considerably lower. It can be bitterly cold in the highlands. If you are planning to stay there for a lengthy period or go hiking, you should take a warm jacket with you. It is also a good idea to have a rain jacket as there are regular showers in the mountains.

WOMEN

Unfortunately, women travelling alone are frequently victims of sexual harassment by local men. You should therefore avoid wearing revealing clothing and walks along lonely beaches and deserted streets. It is a also a good idea to avoid any groups of drunken men you might come across and sit next to local women in crowded buses and trains. Also see our advice (under Dos & Don'ts) on the so-called 'beach boys'.

WEATHER IN COLOMBO

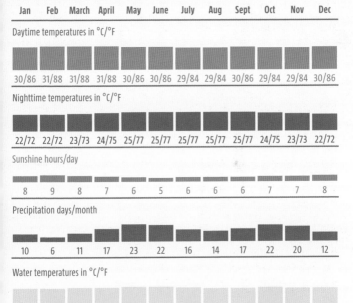

	Jan	Feb	March	April	May	June	July	Aug	Sept	Oct	Nov	Dec
Daytime temperatures in °C/°F	30/86	31/88	31/88	31/88	30/86	30/86	29/84	29/84	30/86	29/84	29/84	30/86
Nighttime temperatures in °C/°F	22/72	22/72	23/73	24/75	25/77	25/77	25/77	25/77	25/77	24/75	23/73	22/72
Sunshine hours/day	8	9	8	7	6	5	6	6	6	7	7	8
Precipitation days/month	10	6	11	17	23	22	16	14	17	22	20	12
Water temperatures in °C/°F	27/81	27/81	28/82	28/82	29/84	29/84	28/82	27/81	27/81	28/82	27/81	27/81

NOTES

MARCO POLO TRAVEL GUIDES

- PACKED WITH INSIDER TIPS
- BEST WALKS AND TOURS
- FULL-COLOUR PULL-OUT MAP
  AND STREET ATLAS

ROAD ATLAS

The green line ▬▬ indicates the Trips & Tours (p. 100–105)
The blue line ▬▬ indicates The perfect route (p. 30–31)

All tours are also marked on the pull-out map

Photo: Dambulla Golden Temple

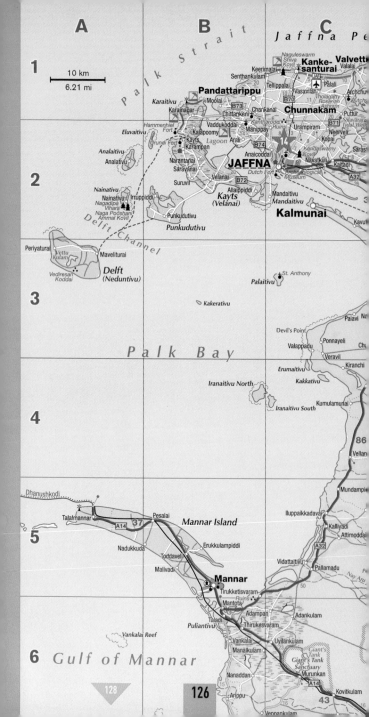

1

10 km
6.21 mi

Palk Strait

Nagulesvarm
Shiva Koyil   **Kanke-**   **Valvett**
Keerimalai   **santurai**   Valalai
Senthankulam   Tholagatty   **Pālali**
Rosann   Archch

Karaitivu
Karainagar   Moolai   B73   Chankanai   Vasavilan   Puttur   B71   Neerveli
Pandattarippu   Chittankeni   Tellippalai   **Chunnakam**   Urampiram

Hammenhiel   Vaddukoddai   Manippay   Kantharodai   Kopai
Fort   Kalapoomy   Ruins
Eluvaitivu   Kayts   Arali
Brunei Fort   Karampan   B74   Anaicoddai

Analaitivu
Analaitivu   Narantanai   Saravanai   **JAFFNA**   Kendasvamy
Suruvil   Velanai   B72   Dutch Fort   Navatkuli

2

Nainativu
Nainativu   Iruppiddi   Allaippiddi   *Mandaitivu*
Nagadipa   Vihara   *Kayts*   **Mandaitivu**
Naga Pooshani   (Velánai)
Ammal Kovil   Punkudutivu   **Kalmunai**

Delft Channel   *Punkudutivu*   Kavu

Periyaturai   Vettu   Mavelturai
Kulam
Delft   St. Anthony
Vediresan   (Neduntivu)   *Palaitivu*
Koddai

3

Kakerativu   Paiavi   Na

Devil's Point   Ponnayeli   Chu
Valappadu
Veravil

P a l k   B a y   *Erumaitivu*   Kiranchi

Iranaitivu North   *Kakkativu*

Iranaitivu South   Kumulamunai

4

86
Vellan

Dhanushkodi   Mundampi

Talalmannar   Pesalai   *Mannar Island*   Iluppaikkadava
A14   37   Kalliyadi
Attimoddai
Nadukkuda   Erukkulampiddi   A32
Toddaveli   Vidattaltivu
Malivadi   Pallamadu

5

Mannar   Nay Aru
Tirukketisvaram   50
Mantota   Ruins
Taladi   Adampan   Adankulam
Puliantivu   Thirukesvaram

Vankalai Reef   Vankalai   Uyilankulam
Manalkulam   Giant's
6   *G u l f   o f   M a n n a r*   Tank   Giant's
Nanaddan   Tank
Sanctuary
Murunkan
A14
▽ 128   **126**   Aripu   43   Kovitkulam
16   Vennankulam

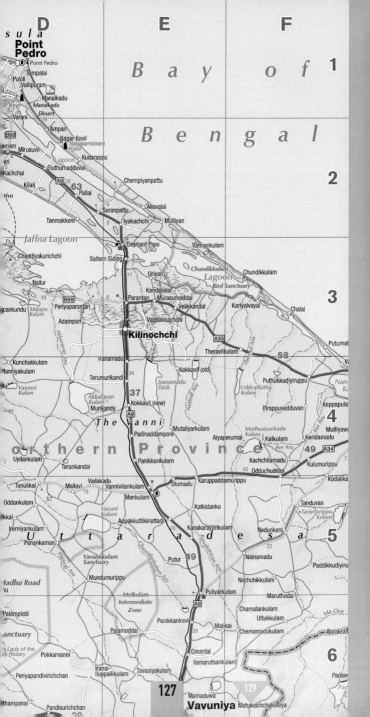

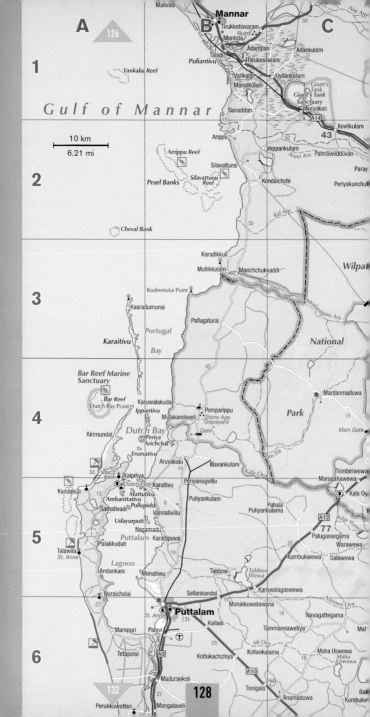

△ 126

Nav Aru

1

Malivadi

Mannar

Tirukketisvaram

Ruins • Mantota

Adampan

50

Adankulam

Taladi

Puliantivu

Thirukesvaram

Vankalai Reef

Vankalai

Manalkulam

Uyilankulam

23

Giant's Tank

Giant's Tank Sanctuary

Murunkan

G u l f   o f   M a n n a r

Nanaddan

15

A14

43

Kovitkulam

10 km

6.21 mi

Arippu

Veppankulam

16

2

Paray

Aruvi Aru

Pannaweddúvan

Arippu Reef

Silavatturai

Periyakunchu

Pearl Banks

Silavatturai Reef

Kondaichchi

30

Kal Aru

Cheval Bank

Karadikkuli

Mullikkulam

Marichchukkaddi

Wilpa

3

Kudremalai Point

Kaaradumunai

Portugal Bay

Pallugaturai

Modaragam Aru

National

Karaitivu

42

Bar Reef Marine Sanctuary

4

Bar Reef

Dutch Bay Point

Karuwalakuda

Ippantivu

Pomparippu

Stone Age Graveyard

Mardanmaduwa

Park

15

Mulakandaveli

Gate

Kirimundal

Dutch Bay

Periya Arichchal

Main Gate

Erumativu

Aruvakalu

Ilavankulam

Kala Oya

14

St. Peter's

Kelk

Kalpitiya

Karaitivu

Periyanagvillu

Can Ela

Thimbiriwewa

Maragahawewa

Kandakuli

13

Dutch Fort

Mattutivu

6

Puliyankulam

Pahala Puliyankulama

A12

Kala Oy

5

Ambanttativu

Pullupiddi

Vannativillu

77

Palugassegama

Samativadi

Udayurputi

Warawewa

Galawewa

Nagamadu

Karadipuval

Soby Wewa

Talawila

St. Anna

Puttalam

Palakkudah

19

33

Kumbukwewa

Lagoon

Andankani

Monativu

Tabbow

Tabbow Wewa

Karuwalagaswewa

Nuraicholai

27

Sellankandal

Nannen Oya

14

Murukkuwatawana

18

Navagattegama

Mal

St. Anne

Puttalam

(3)

Kalladi

Tammannawetiya

6

Mampuri

Palavi

23

Mi Oya

Kollankulama

Maha Usuwewa

Maha Uswewa

Tetapolai

A3

Kottukachchiya

A10

16

△ 132

Maduránkoli

128

Tonigala

Anamaduwa

Bal

Kumbuk

27

Perukkuwattan

Mangalaveli

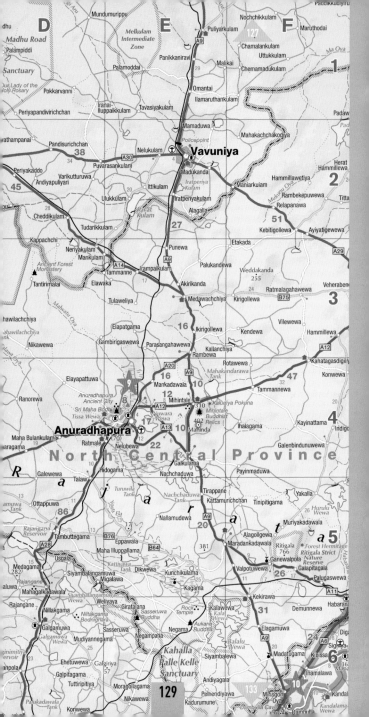

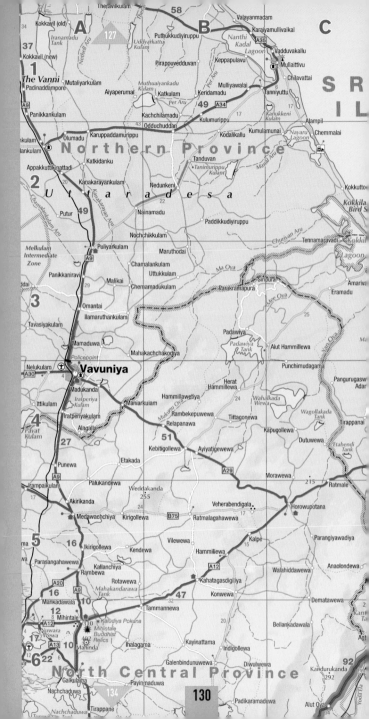

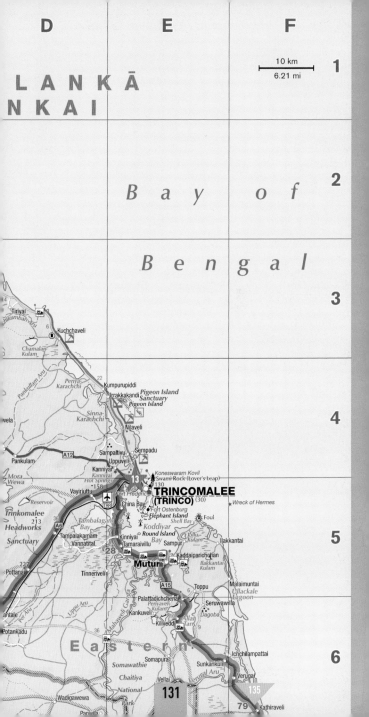

10 km
6.21 mi

L A N K Ā
N K A I

B a y   o f

B e n g a l

Tiriyai
Jakumbah Aru

Kuchchaveli

Chamalan
Kulam

Penya
Karachchi

22

Kumpurupiddi

Irrakkakandi

Pigeon Island
Sanctuary
Pigeon Island

Sinna-
Karachchi

Nilaveli

Pankullam Aru

vela

Pankulam

A12

Sampaltivu

Uppuveli

Sempadu

6

Mora
Wewa

Kanniyai

Kanniyai
Hot Springs
• 158

Vayiriuttu

13

Koneswaram Kovil
Swami Rock (Lover's Leap)

130

TRINCOMALEE
(TRINCO) (30)

Fort Frederic

China Bay

Fort Ostenburg

Wreck of Hermes

Reservoir

Trinkomalee
213
Headworks

Sanctuary

Tambalagam
Bay

22

Elephant Island
Shell Bay

Koddiyar
Round Island
Bay

Foul

A6

Tampalakamam

Vannatital

Kinniyai

Tamaraivillu

Sampur

Villu-
Kulam

Ilakkantai

227

Pottanai

28

Tinneriveli

Muturu

Kaddaiparichchan

Ilakkantai
Kulam

ntale

Uppu Aru

A15

Toppu

Malaimuntai
Ullackale
Lagoon

Palattadichchenai

Pernyeli
Kulam

Seruwawilla

Potankadu

Kankuveli

36

Kiliveddi

Allai
Tank

Dagoba

E a s t e r n

Somapura

Somawathie

Vellai

Sunkankuli

Verugal Aru

Ichchilampattai

Verugal

Chaitiya

National

131

135

79

Kathiraveli

Wadigawewa

Park

Panwila

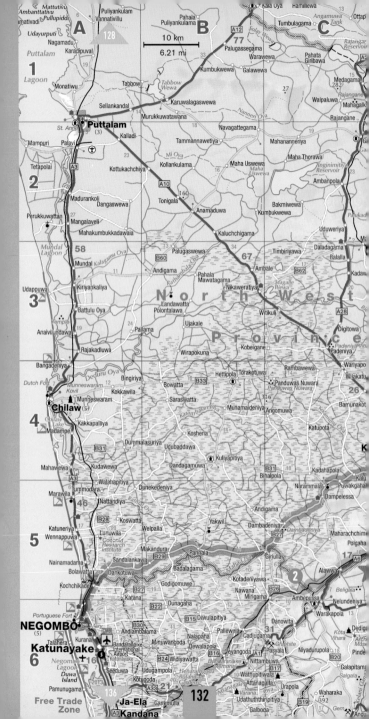

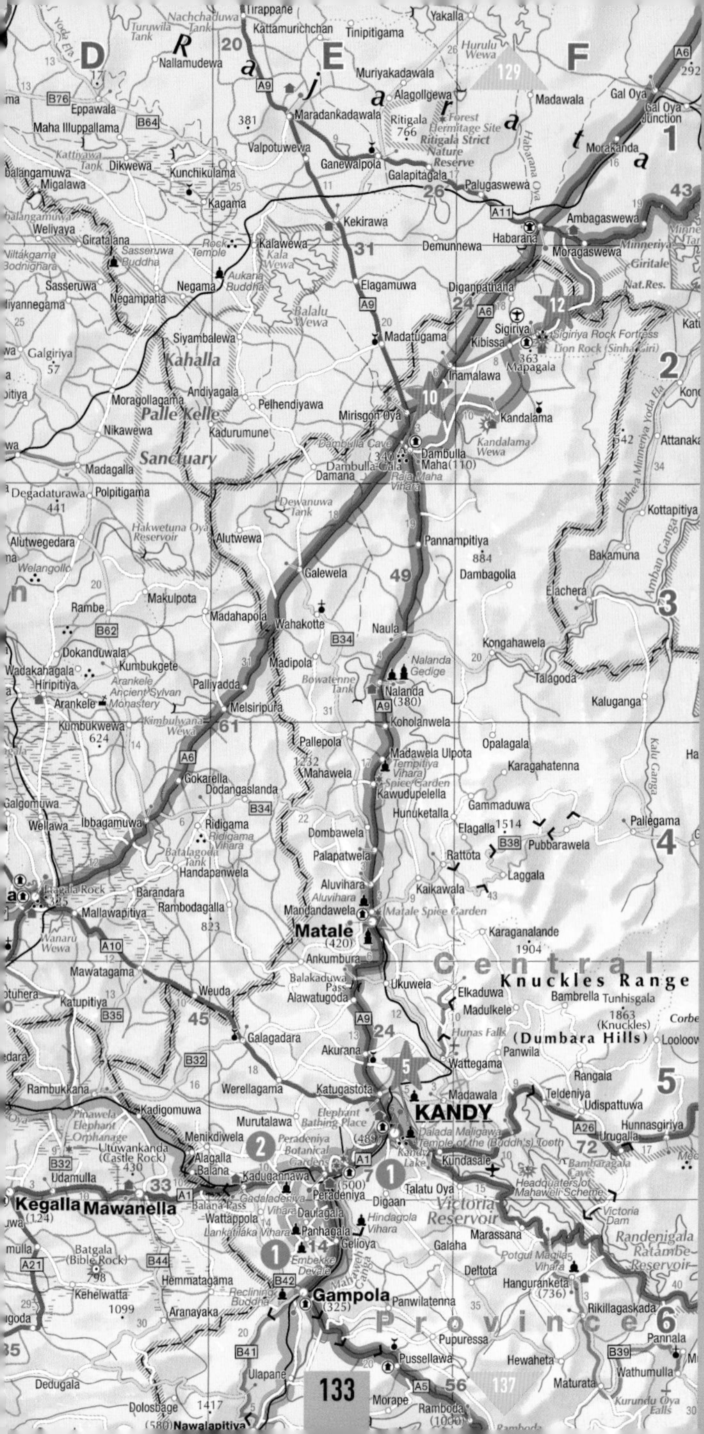
D
E
F
R a j a r a t a
Tirappane
Nachchaduwa Tank
Turuwila Tank
Kattamurichchan
Tinipitigama
Yakalla
Hurulu Wewa
129
Nallamudewa
Muriyakadawala
Alagollgewa
Madawala
Gal Oya
Gal Oya Junction
A6
292
Eppawala
B76
B64
Maha Illuppallama
Maradankadawala
Ritigala 766
Forest Hermitage Site
Ritigala Strict Nature Reserve
Habarana Oya
Morakanda
1
Valpotuwewa
Ganewalpola
Kattiyawa Tank
Dikwewa
Kunchikulama
Galapitagala
Palugaswewa
Balangamuwa
Migalawa
Kagama
26
43
A11
Ambagaswewa
Kekirawa
Weliyaya
Giratalana
Sasseruwa Buddha
Rock Temple
Kalawewa
Kala Wewa
31
Demunnewa
Habarana
Moragaswewa
Minneriya
Giritale
Nat. Res.
Sasseruwa
Negampaha
Negama
Aukana Buddha
Elagamuwa
Diganpathaha
Balalu Wewa
A9
24
12
Sigiriya
Kibissa
Sigiriya Rock Fortress
Lion Rock (Sinha Giri)
363
Mapagala
Siyambalewa
Madatugama
Galgiriya 57
Kahalla
Inamalawa
2
Andiyagala
Moragollagama
Palle Kelle
Pelhendiyawa
Mirisgon Oya
10
Kandalama
Nikawewa
Kadurumune
Sanctuary
Dambulla Cave
340
Dambulla
Maha (110)
Dambulla Gala
Damana
Raja Maha Vihara
Kandalama Wewa
542
Attanaka
Madagalla
Degadaturawa
Polpitigama
441
Dewanuwa Tank
Ellahera Minneriya Yoda Ela
Kottapitiya
Hakwetuna Oya Reservoir
Alutwewa
Alutwegedara
Pannampitiya
884
Welangolla
Galewela
49
Dambagolla
Bakamuna
Amban Ganga
Elachera
3
Rambe
Makulpota
Madahapola
Wahakotte
Naula
B62
B34
Kongahawela
Dokanduwala
Wadakahagala
Kumbukgete
Hiripitiya
Arankele Ancient Sylvan Monastery
Arankele
Madipola
Palliyadda
Bowatenne Tank
Nalanda Gedige
Nalanda (380)
Talagoda
Kaluganga
Melsiripura
Kumbukwewa 624
Kimbulwana Wewa
61
Koholanwela
Pallepola
Opalagala
Kalu Ganga
A6
1232
Mahawela
Madawela Ulpota
Tempitiya Vihara
Spice Garden
Karagahatenna
Gokarella
Dodangaslanda
Kawudupelella
B34
Galgomuwa
Gammaduwa
Hunuketalla
Wellawa
Ibbagamuwa
Ridigama
Ridigama Vihara
Elagalla 1514
B38
Pubbarawela
Pallegama
4
Dombawela
Batalagoda Tank
Handapanwela
Palapatwela
Rattota
Laggala
Elagala Rock
325
Barandara
Aluvihara
Aluvihara
Kaikawala
Mallawapitiya
Rambodagalla
Mandandawela
Matale Spice Garden
823
Matale
(420)
Karaganalande
1904
Wanaru Wewa
A10
Ankumbura
Central
Knuckles Range
Mawatagama
Balakaduwa Pass
Ukuwela
Elkaduwa
Bambrella
Tunhisgala
Potuhera
Katupitiya
Weuda
Alawatugoda
Madulkele
1863 (Knuckles)
Corbet
B35
45
A9
24
Hunas Falls
(Dumbara Hills)
Looloow
Galagadara
Akurana
Panwila
B32
5
Wattegama
Rangala
5
Rambukkana
Werellagama
Katugastota
Madawala
Teldeniya
Udispattuwa
Kadigomuwa
Murutalawa
Elephant Bathing Place
KANDY
A26
Hunnasgiriya
Pinawela Elephant Orphanage
Menikdiwela
(489)
Dalada Maligawa
Temple of the (Buddh's) Tooth
Urugalla
72
Utuwankanda (Castle Rock)
430
2
Peradeniya Botanical Gardens
Kandy Lake
Kundasale
Bambaragala Cave
B32
Udamulla
Alagalla
Balana
Kadugannawa
A1
(500)
1
Headquaters of Mahaweli Scheme
33
A1
Gadaladeniya
Peradeniya
Digaan
Talatu Oya
Victoria Reservoir
Victoria Dam
Kegalla
(124)
Mawanella
Balana Pass
Vihara
Daulagala
Hindagola Vihara
Wattappola
Lankatilaka Vihara
Panhagala
Marassana
Randenigala
Rantambe Reservoir
14
Gelioya
Galaha
Batgala (Bible Rock)
798
1
Embekke Devale
Potgul Magila Vihara
A21
B44
Mahaweli Ganga
Deltota
Hemmatagama
B42
Hanguranketa
(736)
Kehelwatta
1099
Reclining Buddha
Gampola
(325)
Panwilatenna
Aranayaka
Rikillagaskada
Province
6
Pupuressa
Pannala
B41
Pusselawa
B39
Hewaheta
Ulapane
Wathumulla
Dedugala
56
137
Maturata
Morape
A5
Dolosbage
1417
Ramboda
(1000)
Kurundu Oya Falls
(580)
Nawalapitiya

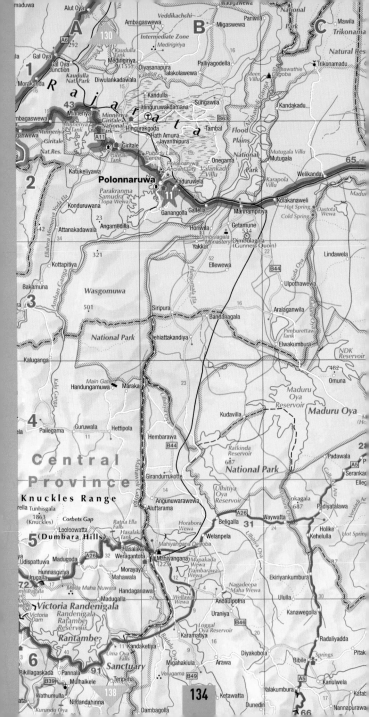

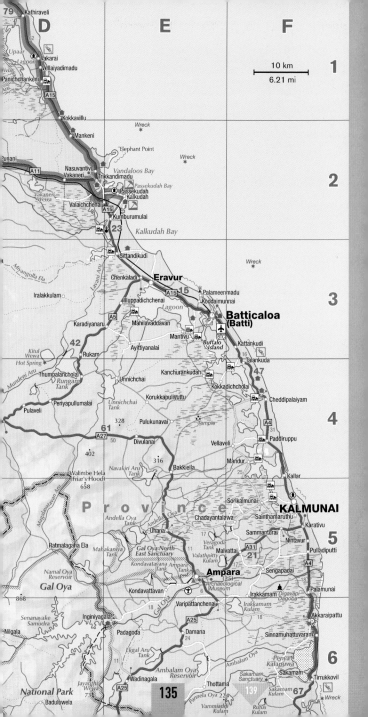

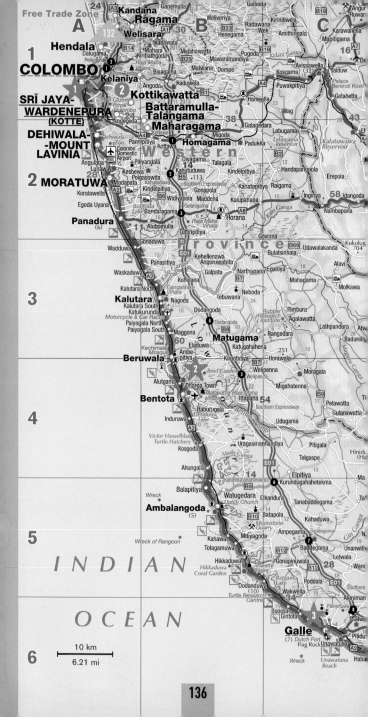

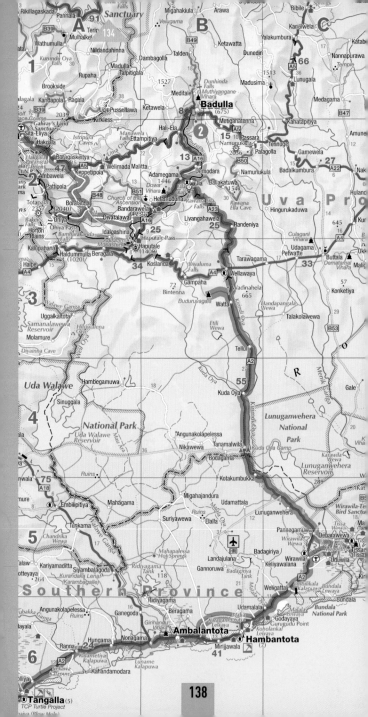

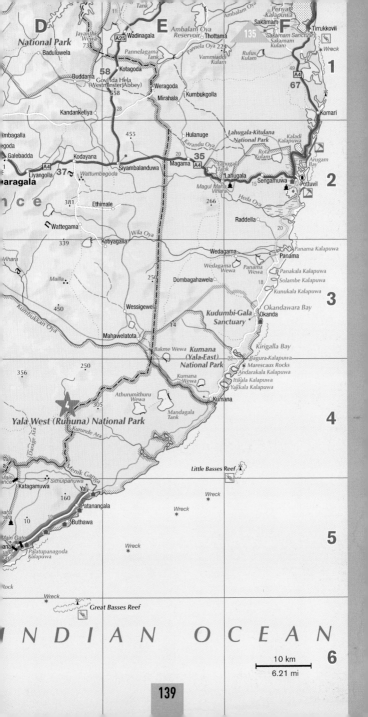

KEY TO ROAD ATLAS

Motorway with junctions	Autobahn mit Anschlussstellen
Motorway under construction	Autobahn in Bau
Toll station	Mautstelle
Roadside restaurant and hotel	Raststätte mit Übernachtung
Roadside restaurant	Raststätte
Filling-station	Tankstelle
Dual carriage-way with motorway characteristics with junction	Autobahnähnliche Schnellstraße mit Anschlussstelle
Trunk road	Fernverkehrsstraße
Thoroughfare	Durchgangsstraße
Important main road	Wichtige Hauptstraße
Main road	Hauptstraße
Secondary road	Nebenstraße
Railway	Eisenbahn
Car-loading terminal	Autozug-Terminal
Mountain railway	Zahnradbahn
Aerial cableway	Kabinenschwebebahn
Railway ferry	Eisenbahnfähre
Car ferry	Autofähre
Shipping route	Schifffahrtslinie
Route with beautiful scenery	Landschaftlich besonders schöne Strecke
Tourist route	Touristenstraße
Closure in winter	Wintersperre
Road closed to motor traffic	Straße für Kfz gesperrt
Important gradients	Bedeutende Steigungen
Not recommended for caravans	Für Wohnwagen nicht empfehlenswert
Closed for caravans	Für Wohnwagen gesperrt
Important panoramic view	Besonders schöner Ausblick

Alleenstr.

XI-V

8%

Wartenstein *Umbalfälle*	Of interest: culture - nature Sehenswert: Kultur - Natur
Bathing beach	Badestrand
National park, nature park	Nationalpark, Naturpark
Prohibited area	Sperrgebiet
Church	Kirche
Monastery	Kloster
Palace, castle	Schloss, Burg
Mosque	Moschee
Ruins	Ruinen
Lighthouse	Leuchtturm
Tower	Turm
Cave	Höhle
Archaeological excavation	Ausgrabungsstätte
Youth hostel	Jugendherberge
Isolated hotel	Allein stehendes Hotel
Refuge	Berghütte
Camping site	Campingplatz
Airport	Flughafen
Regional airport	Regionalflughafen
Airfield	Flugplatz
National boundary	Staatsgrenze
Administrative boundary	Verwaltungsgrenze
Check-point	Grenzkontrollstelle
Check-point with restrictions	Grenzkontrollstelle mit Beschränkung
ROMA	Capital Hauptstadt
VENEZIA	Seat of the administration Verwaltungssitz
Trips & Tours	Ausflüge & Touren
Perfect route	Perfekte Route
MARCO POLO Highlight	MARCO POLO Highlight

INDEX

This index lists all places and destinations plus the names of important people and keywords featured in this guide. Numbers in bold indicate a main entry.

WRITE TO US

e-mail: info@marcopologuides.co.uk

Did you have a great holiday? Is there something on your mind? Whatever it is, let us know! Whether you want to praise, alert us to errors or give us a personal tip – MARCO POLO would be pleased to hear from you. We do everything we can to provide the very latest information for your trip.

Nevertheless, despite all of our authors' thorough research, errors can creep in. MARCO POLO does not accept any liability for this. Please contact us by e-mail or post.

MARCO POLO Travel Publishing Ltd Pinewood, Chineham Business Park Crockford Lane, Chineham Basingstoke, Hampshire RG24 8AL United Kingdom

PICTURE CREDITS
Cover photograph: Fishermen near Negombo, vario images/RHPL
©iStockphoto.com: microgen (16 bottom), webphotographee (17 top); AOD (17 bottom); DuMont Bildarchiv: Kiedrowski/Schwarz (51, 68, 109); Getty Images: Flickr (Dhammika Heenpella/The Images of Sri Lanka) (98); Getty Images: Flickr (Poorfish) (3 bottom, 96/97); Huber: Damm (2 centre bottom, 12/13, 46/47, 102), Picture Finders (5, 29), Ribani (128/129); V. Janicke (48, 111, 113); H. Jennerich (front flap right); G. Jung (83); Laif: Bibel (59), Eisermann (front flap left, 2 centre top, 3 top, 3 centre, 24/25, 32/33, 72, 74/75, 88/89, 115, 141), Emmler (28, 30 right, 34, 55, 71, 90, 100/101, 106/107), Matthes (84), H. Lange (22, 110/111, 114 bottom); look: Acquadro (2 top, 4, 15); K. Maeritz (2 bottom, 18/19, 36/37, 60/61, 104, 112, 112/113); Heiko Marquardt, frischefotos Berlin (1 bottom); mauritius images: age (30 left, 52, 57), Baumgärtner (26 right), ib (Allgöwer) (9), ib (Tack) (58), Mattes (6), Pacific Stock (26 left), Rosenfeld (27), Schön (10/11, 62), Torino (8); MIA (16 centre); PhotoPress: JBE (41, 42, 86); THE KULU SAFARI COMPANY (16 top); M. Thomas (7, 20, 38, 45, 64, 66, 76, 78, 80, 93, 95, 110, 114 top)

1st Edition 2015
Worldwide Distribution: Marco Polo Travel Publishing Ltd, Pinewood, Chineham Business Park, Crockford Lane, Basingstoke, Hampshire RG24 8AL, United Kingdom. E-mail: sales@marcopolouk.com
© MAIRDUMONT GmbH & Co. KG, Ostfildern
Chief editor: Marion Zorn
Author: Bernd Schiller, co-author: Martin H. Petrich, editor: Cordula Natusch
Programme supervision: Ann-Katrin Kutzner, Nikolai Michaelis
Picture editors: Gabriele Forst, Iris Kaczmarczyk
What's hot: wunder media, München
Cartography road atlas & pull-out map: © MAIRDUMONT, Ostfildern
Design: milchhof : atelier, Berlin; Front cover, pull-out map cover, page 1: factor product münchen
Translated from German by Robert Scott McInnes; editor of the English edition: Margaret Howie, fullproof.co.za
Prepress: M. Feuerstein, Wigel
Phrase book in cooperation with Ernst Klett Sprachen GmbH, Stuttgart, Editorial by Pons Wörterbücher

All rights reserved. No part of this book may be reproduced, stored in a retrieval system or transmitted in any form or by any means (electronic, mechanical, photocopying, recording or otherwise) without prior written permission from the publisher.
Printed in China.

DOS & DON'TS

A few things to bear in mind while in Sri Lanka

DON'T SUNBATHE TOPLESS

Nudity and topless bathing are taboo in Sri Lanka, it is also inappropriate to wear T-shirts without a bra and hot pants are also frowned upon. By dressing modestly you will avoid offending the customs and sense of decency of the Sri Lankans.

DO AVOID THE 'BEACH BOYS'

Most people going for a stroll on the beach just think of them as simply annoying. But some female holidaymakers find the self-assured young men who never stop smiling charming. However, the pushy and persistent boys have one main interest: your money! The best thing to do is to ignore them and tell them – politely but firmly – to be on their way.

DON'T PAY OVER THE ODDS

Sri Lankans know that tourists will haggle and they therefore set their prices even higher. At all times try to retain a sense of proportion and remember that no matter how tight your budget is, you will always be far better off than the locals. Those few extra rupees will make a big difference in their lives.

DO BE QUIET

Singhalese and Tamils speak softly and laugh a lot. That cannot understand that their guests think they can achieve something by raising their voice and waving their hands around.

DON'T ENCOURAGE CHILDREN TO BEG

Even if the village children tug at your heart strings, don't give them sweets or money. Instead, give teachers and educational institutions ballpoint pens and coloured pencils (your driver or tour guide will help you). In this way, you will not contribute to the cycle of dependence: children play truant to carry out this lucrative part-time job and later try to earn a living by begging. It is a better idea to help a local aid programme.

DO BE SENSITIVE TO RELIGIOUS ETIQUETTE

Remember that when talking a photograph you should always request permission with a restrained gesture. Naturally, you should only enter sacred places (including the ruins in Polonnaruwa and Anuradhapura) appropriately dressed. In temples, your arms and legs must be covered, your head bare and no shoes! And never stand next to a statue of Buddha to be photographed. That is a punishable offence in Sri Lanka!

DO BEWARE OF HOT CURRIES

Sri Lanka curry can be very fiery; if you do eat something that is too hot don't reach for the water bottle as it will only add to your discomfort. The best way to relieve the pain is to eat some rice or bread and then something neutral. Everything will soon be ok again!